E P I P H A N Y

**INTERPRETING
THE LESSONS OF
THE CHURCH YEAR**

GAIL R. O'DAY

**PROCLAMATION 5
SERIES C**

FORTRESS PRESS MINNEAPOLIS

PROCLAMATION 5
Interpreting the Lessons of the Church Year
Series C, Epiphany

Cover and interior design: Spangler Design Team

Library of Congress Cataloging-in-Publication Data
(Revised for volume C, 2)

Proclamation 5.

   Contents: ser. A. [1] Advent/Christmas / Mark Allan
Powell — [2] Epiphany / Pheme Perkins — [etc.] —
ser. C. [2] Epiphany / Gail R. O'Day
   1. Bible—Homiletical use.   2. Bible—Liturgical
lessons, English.   I. Perkins, Pheme.
BS534.5.P765   1994   251   92-22973
ISBN 0-8006-4193-0 (ser. C, Advent/Christmas)
ISBN 0-8006-4194-9 (ser. C, Epiphany)
ISBN 0-8006-4195-7 (ser. C, Lent)
ISBN 0-8006-4196-5 (ser. C, Holy Week)

The paper used in this publication meets the minimum requirements of American National Standard for Information Sciences—Permanence of Paper for Printed Library Materials, ANSI Z329.48-1984.   ∞™

Manufactured in the U.S.A.   AF 1-4194

98   97   96   95   94   1   2   3   4   5   6   7   8   9   10

CONTENTS

The Epiphany of Our Lord

Lutheran	Roman Catholic	Episcopal	Revised Common
Isa. 60:1-6	Isa. 60:1-6	Isa. 60:1-6, 9	Isa. 60:1-6
Eph. 3:2-12	Eph. 3:2-3a, 5-6	Eph. 3:1-12	Eph. 3:1-12
Matt. 2:1-12	Matt. 2:1-12	Matt. 2:1-12	Matt. 2:1-12

The Epiphany of Our Lord marks the beginning of a new season in the life of the church, a season that celebrates the manifestation of God in Jesus to the world. The feast of the Epiphany is not a postscript to the Christmas season (although the tendency to conflate the Lukan shepherd story and the Matthean magi story often suggests this), but is indeed the beginning of something new. The hidden is revealed, darkness is transformed to light, because of the appearance of God. The significance of this new beginning is reinforced by the way the subsequent Sundays of the season are named: the First, Second (and so on) Sunday *after the Epiphany*. The manifestation of God at Epiphany is the decisive theological reality for the season.

FIRST LESSON: ISAIAH 60:1-6

The central theological themes of the Epiphany feast are: (1) the manifestation of the light of God; and (2) the coming of the Gentile world to this light. The starting point for both these themes is in the Old Testament lesson, Isa. 60:1-6. Isaiah 60:1-6 is a poem addressed to Jerusalem that celebrates the restoration of that city after the Babylonian exile. It does not simply look forward to restoration (as the poems of Isaiah 40–55 do), but reflects on the restoration that is now under way. The poem exhorts Jerusalem to embrace its new life. The exhortation is in two parts: vv. 1-3 ("Arise, shine") and vv. 4-6 ("Lift up your eyes and look around").

Verses 1-3 are dense with language and images of light and radiance. In the Old Testament (e.g., Exod. 24:15-18; 34:29-35), to speak of the glory of the Lord was to speak of God's visible radiance, the shining manifestation of God's power and presence. The images of light and glory in vv. 1 and 2 therefore announce the same event: God's presence is visible in Jerusalem. The light of God's presence distinguishes Jerusalem and its inhabitants from the dark places of the earth and the other people who live in darkness (v. 2). The poem therefore exhorts Jerusalem to mirror in its behavior what God has already done for them: to arise and shine. The promise of v. 3 is extraordinary, given the history of exile. During the exile, Jerusalem's inhabitants went away, outcasts living in other nations and ruled by other kings. But now, because of the radiance of God's presence, nations and kings will come to Jerusalem. Jerusalem has what the peoples of the earth do not have: the light of the Lord.

The exhortations with which v. 4a begins ("Lift up your eyes and look around") build on the images of light and glory from vv. 1-3. Because the darkness has ended, it is now possible for Jerusalem to see. The exhortations also seem to acknowledge the extraordinariness of the reality celebrated in v. 3: Jerusalem must witness the effects of the light with its own eyes.

What Jerusalem sees when it looks is the breadth of the restoration and the gathering of the nations promised in v. 3. In v. 4b, Jerusalem's own families are restored to it and the sight of the returning sons and daughters gives Jerusalem its own radiance (v. 5a). Jerusalem shines with joy. The Hebrew of v. 5a expresses this joy with a poignant metaphor, "your heart . . . shall be enlarged" (KJV).

In vv. 5b and 6 Jerusalem's material possessions are restored to it, and then some. By ship ("the abundance of the sea") and by caravan ("a multitude of camels"), from the far reaches of the world (Midian and Ephah are eastern Arabian trading regions), the wealth of the nations is brought to Jerusalem. The gifts include gold and frankincense (v. 6; see Matt. 2:11); gold to restore the temple treasury, frankincense (for anointings) to restore the liturgical life of the temple. (Verse 9, an additional verse included in the Episcopal lectionary, replays the dynamics of restoration from vv. 4b-6 but points explicitly to the return of family and wealth from western regions across the Mediterranean.) It is interesting to note that when Job's life is restored to him after his struggle with God, the restoration involves the same elements as in Isaiah 60: family and wealth (Job 42:10-17).

The nations bring their wealth to Jerusalem as an act of praise to Jerusalem's God (v. 6). The restoration of Jerusalem is thus a personal (family) and social (wealth) act that has religious and political implications. Jerusalem is positioned as the center of the world because of the manifest radiance of God that shines from within it.

GOSPEL: MATTHEW 2:1-12

Matthew used the Isaiah 60 text as the lens through which he viewed the manifestation of God in Christ, and the church has long acknowledged that linkage by pairing Isa. 60:1-6 and Matt. 2:1-12 as lessons for the Feast of the Epiphany. The influence of Isaiah 60 on Matt. 2:1-12 is evident in textual details (e.g., the gold and frankincense of v. 11), but more importantly in the theological themes that shape Matthew's picture of the revelation of Jesus to the world. As in Isaiah 60, the Gentile world is drawn to God by the radiance of light.

The arrival of the "wise men from the East" in Matt. 2:1 indicates that the story of Jesus is not a parochial event, limited to Judea and Jerusalem, but is played out on the world stage. Christians are so familiar with pageant versions of the story of the wise men and the star that it is easy to overlook the tension that characterizes Matthew's telling of the story. The wise men's mission and question is politically charged (v. 2): They come to the capital city of the Jews, the domain of King Herod, and ask for the location of the King of the Jews in order to pay him homage, when by rights it is Herod to whom visiting dignitaries should be paying homage. Is it any wonder that King Herod and all the inhabitants of Jerusalem are frightened (v. 3)? Herod's kingship is placed in jeopardy by the wise men's request.

Matthew's use of the noun "king" in 2:1-12 (and continuing into 2:13-23) reveals the threat the wise men pose. There is a heavy concentration of the use of "king" in vv. 1-3 (twice with Herod's name, vv. 1, 3; once of Jesus, v. 2). After v. 3, however, Matthew will never again refer to Herod as King Herod. He is referred to once anonymously as "the king" (v. 9), but more significantly, is referred to everywhere else simply as "Herod" (vv. 7, 12, 13, 15, 16, 19, 22). Matthew the storyteller thus de facto strips Herod of his kingship, confirming that a new king is on the scene.

Herod's frightened response is to summon the religious authorities and inquire about the Messiah (v. 4). This marks a fascinating turn in the story. First, the wise men inquired after the "king," using secular, political terminology; Herod inquires after the "Messiah," the ruler in religious, political terminology. Second, the religious authorities' answer (vv. 5 and 6) is given in the language of prophecy. Matthew's use of Micah 5:2, 4 here positions the birth of Jesus as the fulfillment of God's promises to Israel. Jesus' birth in Bethlehem marks him as the ruler in the Davidic line, the shepherd of God's people whose claim to kingship rests on more than appointment under Roman rule. As in Isaiah 60, Matthew 2 shows that the manifestation of God in the world is both a religious and political drama.

Verses 7-8 are an excellent example of how narrative restraint can build suspense. Matthew depicts Herod as presenting himself as at one with the wise men's desires, sharing their intent to pay homage to the new king. This depiction leaves the reader with many unresolved questions, however, all of which point to Herod's untrustworthiness: Why does Herod meet with the wise men in secret? How could the fear of v. 3 turn so quickly to supportive interest? Why would one king of the Jews want to pay homage to another who is acclaimed by that title (cf. the growing tension in Saul's attitude to David in 1 Samuel)? The conflict of the story is thus joined, and the reader awaits its resolution.

Verses 9-12, then, are not a romantic idyll, an innocent tale of kings bearing gifts, but are the crucial moment in the religious and political drama. (Note that Jesus is not referred to as an infant in these verses, as he is in Luke 2:12 and 16, but as a child, a reminder that the story of the wise men is not a Christmas story but belongs to a later period in the child's life.) The wise men are led to Jesus by the light of the star, and when they find him, they are overwhelmed by joy (v. 10). It is the enactment of Isa. 60:3, "nations shall come to your light and kings to the brightness of your dawn."

The wise men's actions in v. 11 are also an enactment of Isaiah 60. The nations brought gifts to Jerusalem to proclaim their praise of Jerusalem's God (Isa. 60:6), and the wise men from the East now bring the same gifts in order to pay homage to Jesus as king of the Jews. When they pay homage to the child, they acknowledge his sovereignty and the legitimacy of his reign. The gifts of gold and frankincense, as in Isa. 60:6, represent both the wealth of the nations brought to the king (gold) and the fragrances for the anointing of the king (frankincense, myrrh). Jesus as the fulfillment of God's promise to Israel is stated explicitly in the citation of Micah 5 in v. 6; here, Jesus as the fulfillment of God's promises to the nations is stated implicitly in the enactment of Isa. 60:1-6.

The arrival of the wise men thus shows that the good news of God in Christ is available to the nations. The wise men's allegiance to Jesus is complete and providentially governed: They will not return to Herod with the information he requested (v. 12). The story of Jesus is thus not only Israel's story, but is the Gentiles' story as well. Matthew 2:1-12 shows that the Gentiles have been included in the story from the very beginning, and indeed, their inclusion was anticipated and promised by God through the prophets.

SECOND LESSON: EPHESIANS 3:1-12

The language of Eph. 3:1-12 is obviously different from the storytelling in Matt. 2:1-12, but Paul is making the same claim in the Ephesians lesson that Matthew makes with the arrival of the wise men from the East: The inclusion of the Gentiles belongs to God's purpose and promise. The relationship between Jews and Gentiles in the gospel was a crucial issue for early Christians, because resolving that relationship meant reaching a decision about whether non-Jews could be included in the providence of

God contained in God's promises to Israel. Paul approaches the question from two angles in Eph. 3:1-12: God's plan for the Gentiles and Paul's part in that plan.

First, Paul consistently speaks of the inclusion of the Gentiles in terms of God's mystery and God's plan (vv. 3, 4, 5, 9, 11). To contemporary Christians, "mystery" and "plan" may seem almost to be opposites, but for Paul and the Christians of Paul's day they were roughly synonymous. "Mystery" refers to God's plan that has been at work throughout the ages, although its workings have not always been evident to God's people. God's plan is thus a mystery because it has been hidden from human perception, but now, according to Paul, with the inclusion of the Gentiles in the good news of God's presence in Jesus, the mystery is revealed (vv. 3, 5, 9-10). Paul is eloquent in naming the contents of the mystery: "the Gentiles have become fellow heirs, members of the same body, and sharers in the promise in Christ Jesus through the gospel" (v. 6).

It is helpful to read Eph. 3:1-12 in the context of Isa. 60:1-6, because the prophetic text confirms what Paul is saying. The manifestation of God was not limited to Jerusalem and its inhabitants in God's plan, but was available and indeed intended for the nations (Isa. 60:3). Paul, in distinction from Isaiah, locates the specific fulfillment of the promise in Jesus, but the overarching promise of the inclusion of all in God's plan goes back to God's "eternal purpose" (Eph. 3:11).

Second, Paul stresses that his entire ministry, including the imprisonment during which he composes the letter, is for the sake of the inclusion of the Gentiles in the good news of God in Jesus Christ, and that he received that ministry because of the grace of God (vv. 2, 7, 8). The mystery was revealed to him as part of this grace (v. 7). Paul's vocation is "to bring to the Gentiles the news of the boundless riches of Christ" and hence to make God's mystery known to many people (vv. 9-10). Paul's faith and gratitude to the God who has been made manifest to him in Jesus Christ animates this Ephesians passage, and Paul's work is governed by the confidence that this same God is available to all. Paul names the church as one of the carriers of the mystery to others (v. 10). Paul is a "servant" of the mystery (v. 7), so that all may share in God's grace.

Paul's self-description as a servant of the mystery holds the key to the preacher's relationship to these Epiphany lessons. The contemporary preacher, like Paul, is a servant of the mystery also, commissioned by the grace of God to help people see the shape of the mystery of God. These three Epiphany lessons enable the preacher to rediscover God's mystery and to offer that mystery to his or her congregation. In the Epiphany celebration, the church is brought again to the experience of God made manifest in the world, to Jesus as God's light in the world, and to the changes that manifestation makes in the way the world is ordered.

The Baptism of Our Lord
First Sunday after the Epiphany

Lutheran	Roman Catholic	Episcopal	Revised Common
Isa. 42:1-7	Isa. 40:1-5, 9-11	Isa. 42:1-9	Isa. 43:1-7
Acts 10:34-38	Titus 2:11-14; 3:4-7	Acts 10:34-38	Acts 8:14-17
Luke 3:15-17, 21-22	Luke 3:15-16, 21-22	Luke 3:15-16, 21-22	Luke 3:15-17, 21-22

The First Sunday after the Epiphany is also called The Baptism of Our Lord. That liturgical context dictates that the Gospel lesson, the Lukan version of Jesus' baptism, be the guiding text for this Sunday. The Old Testament and Acts lessons provide additional theological commentary on the meaning of Jesus' baptism.

GOSPEL: LUKE 3:15-17, 21-22

The Gospel lesson is divided into two parts: 3:15-17, the teaching of John the Baptist, and 3:21-22, the baptism of Jesus.

As Luke 3:15 makes clear, John the Baptist's preaching led those who heard him to wonder "whether he might be the Messiah." Before looking ahead to what John says in 3:16-17, then, it is important to look back to what John said in 3:7-14 and examine what aroused those Messianic hopes. John issued a far-reaching call to righteousness and right actions (vv. 8, 10-14). John addressed the multitudes as a "brood of vipers" (v. 7; cf. Matt. 3:7, where only the religious leadership is called by this epithet), announcing that the people's religious heritage does not privilege them with God. They must bear fruit to be truly God's children (vv. 8-9). John's teaching is thus a call to repentance and new behavior, reinforced by the eschatological language of fire and judgment. The people's response to John's words in v. 15 provides the reader with an important glimpse into Messianic expectations in Jesus' day. Verse 15 suggests that one clue to the Messiah's presence was the urgent call for a return to lives of fruitfulness and justice, to restored relationships with God and one another.

John does not identify Jesus by name in his response to the people (vv. 16-17). Even though the reader knows that Jesus is the one to whom John the Baptist points, John's words may evoke more of a sense of expectancy for the reader if he or she can hold Jesus' name in abeyance while John speaks and concentrate on John's description. If the reader moves too quickly to name Jesus, the heart of John's words may be overlooked. John also does not give the one of whom he speaks the title "Messiah," even though that would be natural given the subject of the crowd's wonderment. Instead, John allows his description of the one who is coming to provide the answer to the crowd's question, without falling back on names or titles.

At the heart of John's answer is the contrast between himself and the one who is coming, as if to say, "If I have made you wonder about the Messiah, you should see who is coming next." John contrasts both his person and his baptism with the one who is coming. The reader does well to remember the power of John's words in 3:7-14 when hearing John's assertion that "one who is more powerful than I is coming" (v. 16*b*). In order to dramatize this power contrast, John uses the vivid, domestic image of the sandal (v. 16*c*). To untie a man's sandal was the work of a servant, and John, the powerful preacher of repentance, is not even worthy to do a servant's work for this one who comes.

With his secondary status established, John can return to the theme of baptism with which his answer began (v. 16*a*). The difference between the two men's respective baptisms is the ultimate demonstration of the difference between them. John baptizes with water (v. 16*a*), a ritual action of bathing to represent symbolically repentance for forgiveness of sins, the washing away of the old and impure. The one who is coming will baptize with the Holy Spirit and with fire (v. 16*d*). That is, he will baptize with the very agents that effect repentance. His baptism therefore will not be a symbolic enactment of repentance but will be the carrier of life (Spirit) and judgment (fire) that makes repentance possible.

John's words in v. 17 expand on the judgment language in the image of baptism with fire. Verse 17 is consistent with John's teaching about the ax in 3:9, but with a significant advance: what John preached (repentance, judgment), the one who is coming will accomplish. Winnowing was a step in the harvesting of grain. The grain was tossed into the air with a winnowing fork so that the wind could blow away the lighter straw and chaff. The grain would then fall back down at the winnower's feet. The image of winnowing, the separation of wheat and chaff, was a frequent metaphor in the Old Testament to describe the fate of the wicked and unjust (e.g., Ps. 1:4; 35:5; 83:13; Jer. 13:24; 15:7; Isa. 40:24). John's vivid depiction of the winnowing process in v. 17 suggests that the messianic age will be a time of reckoning for the just and the unjust. Who people are will be revealed in the presence of the one who is coming, the one who will satisfy people's messianic wonderments and expectations.

Luke provides a very lean account of Jesus' baptism (vv. 21-22). To be more precise, he provides no account of the *baptism* at all, because v. 21

picks up the narrative account after the baptism ("when Jesus also had been baptized"). Luke also reports Jesus' baptism in the passive voice and makes no mention of John the Baptist's role. Luke's treatment of John distinguishes his account from the baptismal tradition he shares with Mark and Matthew. Both Matthew and Luke struggled to explain why Jesus would have received John's baptism. As the son of God, he did not need a "baptism of repentance for the forgiveness of sins" (Luke 3:3). Matthew resolves the dilemma by including an extended conversation between Jesus and John in which Jesus states the reason he wants to be baptized (because he is faithful to God, Matt. 3:14-15). Luke, by contrast, resolves the dilemma by interrupting the story of John the Baptist and Jesus' baptism to record John the Baptist's arrest (vv. 18-20), an event that comes much later in Matthew (14:3-4) and Mark (6:17-18). By reminding the reader of John's arrest at this juncture, Luke effectively eliminates John from the scene and thereby ends any debate that Jesus was in need of John's baptism. Jesus and God are the only actors at Jesus' baptism in Luke (cf. the baptism account in John 1:29-34). To reinforce the centrality of the relationship between Jesus and God, Luke records that Jesus prayed after his baptism, an overt sign of that relationship.

As in the other synoptic accounts, the aftermath of Jesus' baptism is marked by three signs of God's presence: the opening of heaven, the visible descent of the Holy Spirit, and the voice from heaven. The visible descent of the Holy Spirit serves two purposes. First, it shows that Jesus is the one about whom John spoke in v. 16. Jesus receives the Spirit so that he can baptize with the Spirit (e.g., Acts 1:5). Second, the descent of the Spirit recalls Isa. 42:1, where God's servant is anointed with the Spirit. The descent of the Spirit thus functions as Jesus' anointing for his ministry.

The words that the voice from heaven speaks are a combination of Ps. 2:7 and Isa. 42:1. The words from Isa. 42:1 ("with whom I am well pleased") are words spoken by God to his servant. The words from Ps. 2:7 acknowledge the king of Israel as God's son ("you are my son"). This combination of words at Jesus' baptism provides the decisive christological categories for the baptism story: Jesus' relationship to God (Son) and his vocation (servant). These words are spoken privately to Jesus ("you are . . ."; cf. Matt. 3:17). The public announcement of Jesus' vocation will wait until Jesus' appearance at the synagogue in Nazareth (Luke 4:16-30).

FIRST LESSON: ISAIAH 40:1-5, 9-11; 42:1-9; 43:1-7

The Old Testament lessons for this Sunday differ among the four lectionaries and move the interpretation of Jesus' baptism in two directions.

The Lutheran and Episcopal lectionaries use the Servant Song of Isaiah 42 to focus on the christocentric dimensions of the baptism. The Roman Catholic and Revised Common lectionaries use Isaiah texts that focus more on the community's experience of good news.

Isaiah 42:1-9 consists of two units, vv. 1-4, the Servant Song, and vv. 5-9, a celebration of God as the giver of life and freedom. The pairing of Isa. 42:1-4 with Luke 3:21-22 is a continuation of the theological tradition that is already evident in the Synoptic Gospels themselves; the early Christians saw Jesus' baptism through the lens of this servant song. That is, they understood Jesus' baptism as his anointing for his vocation (Isa. 42:1).

The identity of the servant in this and the other Servant songs (Isa. 49:1-6; 50:4-11; 52:13—53:12) is never made clear. The servant may be an individual or it may be the community of Israel. The poem may be intentionally ambiguous about the identity of this central figure in order to underscore that what the servant does is of primary importance, not who the servant is. Three times in Isa. 42:1-4 the servant's work for justice is mentioned (vv. 1, 3, 4). It is the servant's unflinching work for justice that evokes the resistance that threatens his ministry and, according to later songs, will place his life in peril.

Verses 5-9 describe who this God is who has anointed the servant for the work of justice and what a world lived according to God's justice will include. These verses give content to the servant's work. God is celebrated as the creator, the giver of life to the natural world and to human beings (v. 5). God is the maker and keeper of covenant who calls Israel to share in God's covenanted work of liberation and to extend that work to the nations (vv. 6-7). In v. 8, God reminds Jerusalem that their God is the one true sovereign God (cf. Deut. 4:23-24; 5:6-10). The exile will come to an end and "new things" begin because of the word of this one God (v. 9).

In using Isaiah 42 as a lens through which to interpret Jesus' baptism and the beginning of his ministry, the early Christians chose a theologically powerful text. Isaiah 42 helped them understand Jesus as God's faithful servant for justice who would not falter even when oppressed.

Isaiah 40:1-5, 9-11 (the lesson for the Roman Catholic lectionary) is the opening verses of 2 Isaiah, the poems of hope and promise that the exile will end and restoration begin. The traditional description of John the Baptist as herald (Matthew 3:3; Luke 3:4-6; John 1:23) is drawn from Isa. 40:3-5. The use of that text as a commentary on Jesus' baptism thus places the emphasis on the good news that John announces in his identification of Jesus as the one who is to come. Isaiah 40:3-5, 9 emphasize announcement and preparation for the coming of God; Isa. 40:1-2, 10-11 focus on the content of the announcement and what God's presence will mean: comfort and care. Israel in exile experienced themselves as absent from God. In Isaiah 40 the herald announces the end of the experience of absence, "Here is your God" (40:9).

Isaiah 43:1-7 (Revised Common Lectionary) is a salvation oracle, a word that announces God's presence to exiled Israel (vv. 2, 3, 5); claims Israel as God's own (vv. 1, 4); and banishes Israel's fears with God's presence (vv. 1, 5-7). Read in the context of Jesus' baptism, this text reflects on the effects of that baptism on the community. Jesus' baptism and God's announcement of Jesus as Son and Servant functions as a salvation oracle for the Christian community, a promise of God's presence with them. To read Isa. 43:1-7 this way is, of course, to move outside of its historical setting and original intent as words of hope to Israel in exile, but it is in keeping with its theological vision of ever-new futures in the presence of God.

SECOND LESSON: ACTS 8:14-17; 10:34-38; TITUS 2:11-14; 3:4-7

The second lessons for this Sunday also contain a wide variety of responses to Jesus' baptism, but all four have in common that they deal explicitly with the place of baptism in the life of the church.

The Lutheran and Episcopal lectionaries again share a reading, *Acts 10:34-38* (this reading appears on this Sunday in Year A in the Revised Common Lectionary). Acts 10:34-38 is the beginning of Peter's sermon that follows the story of the baptism of Cornelius, the first Gentile baptized in Acts. In this sermon, Peter identifies Jesus' baptism and John's announcement of that baptism as the beginning of Jesus' ministry (v. 37). The view of Jesus' baptism in Acts 10 is theologically of a piece with Luke 3:15-17, 21-22. Jesus' baptism was his anointing with the Spirit (Acts 10:38; cf. Luke 3:22; Isa. 42:1). As such, it was the inaugural event of his vocation. Acts 10 moves beyond the treatment of the baptism in Luke 3 to identify John's announcement of Jesus' baptism as the beginning of the spread of the gospel message (vv. 36-37). That message bears fruit in the baptism of Cornelius, because the inclusion of a Gentile in the gospel message vividly demonstrates the impartiality of God (vv. 34-35).

The second lesson used in the Revised Common Lectionary is *Acts 8:14-17*, a short narrative of the baptism of the Samaritans. The baptism of the Samaritans marks the fulfillment of one step in Jesus' commission of his disciples at his ascension, ". . . and you will be my witnesses in Jerusalem, in all Judea and *Samaria*, and to the ends of the earth" (Acts 1:8). The Acts 8 narrative demonstrates a central pivot of the Lukan theology of the church: The spread of the Gospel was accompanied by the spread of the Holy Spirit. The truth that John the Baptist preached, that Jesus would baptize with the Holy Spirit and with fire (Luke 3:16), did not end when Jesus' earthly ministry was completed. Rather, Jesus' baptism with the Spirit continues in the work of his followers and is a shaping reality of the church's life.

The Roman Catholic lesson, *Titus 2:11-15; 3:4-7*, is distinct from the other three lectionaries because it is not part of a narrative account (i.e., the Acts story) of baptism and the early church. Rather, it is a theological reflection on the effects of baptism on the baptized community. The theological foundation of both excerpts from Titus is that God's grace has been made available through Jesus Christ (2:11; 3:6-7).

In Titus 2:11-14, the focus is on the changes in community that are possible as a result of God's gift of grace and that serve as a sign of the grace at work in the community. The emphasis of the passage on good deeds recalls John the Baptist's emphasis on good fruit (Luke 3:9-14). Titus 3:4-7 contains an explicit reference to baptism (v. 5) and interprets the "water of rebirth and renewal" as an act of the Holy Spirit. Titus 3:6-7 equates the pouring out of the Spirit at baptism with the pouring out of the grace of Jesus Christ. The community's baptism therefore is the way it experiences God's salvation in Jesus.

Second Sunday after the Epiphany

Lutheran	Roman Catholic	Episcopal	Revised Common
Isa. 62:1-5	Isa. 62:1-5	Isa. 62:1-5	Isa. 62:1-5
1 Cor. 12:1-11	1 Cor. 12:4-11	1 Cor. 12:1-11	1 Cor. 12:1-11
John 2:1-11	John 2:1-11	John 2:1-11	John 2:1-11

The Gospel lesson for this Sunday was read at the Feast of the Epiphany in ancient lectionaries, because the Cana miracle through which Jesus' glory was made manifest (2:11), was recognized as a classic text of Epiphany. The lesson's use on this Sunday in Year C reflects that ancient liturgical practice. The Old Testament lesson is another lesson from Isaiah and continues some themes from the Isaiah lessons at Epiphany and the Baptism of Our Lord—the glory that comes from God to God's people and the joy of Jerusalem's restoration after exile. The epistle lesson does not have any intentional theological overlap with the other lessons; instead it begins a series of semi-continuous readings from 1 Corinthians for the Sundays after Epiphany. In each of the three lectionary cycles, a reading from 1 Corinthians provides the lessons for the Sundays following the Baptism of Our Lord. In Year C readings from 1 Corinthians 12–15 provide the lessons.

GOSPEL: JOHN 2:1-11

John 2:1-11 follows the standard form of a miracle story: vv. 1-5, setting and preparation of the miracle; vv. 6-8, the miracle; vv. 9-11, attestation of the miracle. The setting (vv. 1-2) provides all the main ingredients of a story—place, time, event, cast of characters. The time reference in v. 1 ("on the third day") links the Cana miracle to the call of Jesus' disciples in 1:35-51.

The problem that leads to the miracle is the lack of wine (v. 3). The exchange between Jesus and his mother on the subject of wine (vv. 3-5) is one of the more interesting parts of the story. Jesus' mother requests nothing of him in v. 3, but Jesus' response in v. 4 suggests that he has heard her words as containing an implied request. Jesus' words to his mother in v. 4 may sound harsh or rude to contemporary ears, but they are not. By calling his mother "Woman," he distances himself from any familial claims (cf. Mark 3:33), and the expression, "what concern is that to you and me," is a common Semitic expression of disengagement (cf. 2 Kings 3:13; 2 Chron. 35:21). Jesus' words thus distance himself from his mother, and his reference to his hour in v. 4*b* explain why he does this. "Hour" is used metaphorically in John to refer to the hour of Jesus' glorification, that is, his death, resurrection, and ascension (e.g., 13:1, 17:1). The only claim on Jesus' time or actions is thus the "hour" set for him by God, and all other claims must find their place within the broader claim of his "hour." Jesus' response in v. 4 puts the reader on notice that there may be more here than immediately meets the eye. A comment about the lack of wine at a wedding feast evokes a response about Jesus' death and resurrection.

Interestingly, Jesus' mother does not take Jesus' response as a rebuff or rejection. She seems to understand the reference to his hour, because she expresses confidence in his ability to do something, but turns all control of his actions over to him ("Do whatever he tells you," v. 5).

The focus of vv. 6-8 is on the stone water jars. The jars were probably to be used at the wedding for the ritual washing of hands before the meal. The number of jars and the volume of water they could hold are extravagant, however, more than sufficient even for a large wedding crowd. Lest the reader miss the quantities of water involved in the miracle, v. 7 twice mentions the filling of the jars. The precise moment when the transformation of water into wine occurs is not narrated; instead Jesus' commands before (v. 7) and after (v. 8) are recounted. Jesus' mother was right; Jesus would tell the servants what to do (v. 5).

The first mention of the miraculous transformation is in the description of the beverage the steward drinks, "the water turned into wine" (v. 9). The steward's response to the wine he tastes provides the public attestation to the miracle. The source of the wine is a mystery to the steward. He does not know that it comes from Jesus, as do all good gifts in the Gospel of John. The quality of the wine also puzzles him. The steward's comments to the bridegroom indicate that the wine's goodness exceeds all expectations and conventions (v. 10). "Good wine" has a double meaning. It makes sense on the level of the story line, but it also points to the theological truth of the miracle. In the Old Testament, an abundance of good wine is a symbol of eschatological fulfillment, of the arrival of God's new age (e.g., Joel 3:18). The steward's words about good wine, then, suggest that the miracle is the beginning of something new, the fulfillment of something anticipated ("you have kept the good wine *until now*"). This miracle, which is the inaugural act of Jesus' ministry in John, can also be read as the inauguration of God's promised and much anticipated salvation of God's people.

The Fourth Evangelist's commentary in v. 11 provides the key to interpreting the miracle and the preacher does well to take his or her cue from this verse. The miracle is a "sign," an act that points to something beyond itself. That is, the significance of the miracle does not rest in the miraculous transformation alone, but in what can be seen in and through this act, in what it reveals about Jesus. As a "sign," this miracle points to Jesus' glory, to the manifestation of God in Jesus. This miracle is an epiphany, a revelation of the divine that leads to faith ("the disciples believed in him").

The late twentieth-century preacher may be tempted on the one hand to dismiss the miracle story as primitive, pre-scientific religion, or on the other hand, to fall back on scientific positivism or rationalism and try to explain the miracle. With either strategy, the miracle as epiphany is lost. The important questions are not, "Could or did this happen?" but "Why did the early church remember this story? Why tell this story?" If the preacher is able to focus on those questions, then he or she may be able to experience the epiphany of the story and share that epiphany with a congregation.

The superabundance of good wine at the wedding at Cana is a sign of God's presence in the world in the person of Jesus. The abundance of this miracle of transformation reveals the character of God in Jesus: gracious and life giving. The power of the miracle rests not in the physical feat, but in the glimpse of Jesus' glory, in the taste of God's good grace. The preacher is invited to see what the disciples saw in the miracle, a revelation of God in Christ.

FIRST LESSON: ISAIAH 62:1-5

The juxtaposition of John 2:1-11 and Isa. 62:1-5 on this Sunday provides additional insight into the symbolism of the Gospel lesson. Not only was an abundance of good wine a symbol of eschatological fulfillment in the Old Testament, but the wedding feast was a symbol for God's joy (Isa. 62:5). A wedding feast is thus the appropriate place for this miracle of God's abundant goodness in Jesus to occur.

62:1-5 begins with language quite reminiscent of Isa. 60:1-3. Both use images of light and brightness to describe Jerusalem's vindication (Isa. 60:1 and 62:1); both promise that Jerusalem's light will be visible to the nations (60:3 and 62:2). Whereas Isa. 60:1-6 was framed as the prophet's exhortation to Jerusalem to embrace God's restoration of the city, Isa. 62:1-5 is now addressed both to Jerusalem and to God.

The prophet's insistence in 62:1 on his call to speak is a reminder to the people and to God of God's promises (cf. Isa. 62:6-7). "For the sake of" the city, the prophet will not be silent (v. 1) because too much rides on the city's vindication. The conjunction "until" in v. 1 indicates that the full vindication has not come yet, so the prophet will continue to announce God's promises until those promises become reality. That the prophet is holding God to God's word is evidenced by the echoes of earlier promises in the prophet's words (e.g., 60:1; 52:1-2; 43:1).

Yet the prophet is also holding the people to God's word. The historical reality was that the restoration of Jerusalem after 538 B.C.E. did not go immediately as the people had expected. The reestablishment of the city was accompanied by famine and poverty. The "glory" in this turn of events was hard for the people to see, and the temptation to despair was real. In that context, the prophet speaks an alternative vision, a reminder of who God is and what God promises God's people.

The prophet's words of hope center around three images: a new name (vv. 2b, 4), Jerusalem as a crown of beauty (v. 3), and marriage (v. 5). To receive a new name in Jewish tradition is to receive a new status and identity (e.g., the shift from Abram to Abraham, Gen. 17:5; from Jacob to Israel, Gen. 32:28). The name change envisioned by the prophet for Jerusalem vividly embodies the change from the past of despair to a future of hope. The old names "Forsaken" and "Desolate" (v. 4a) capture Jerusalem's experience of exile: God had forsaken them and their land. The new names convey the opposite experience and capture the change in Jerusalem's reality and relationship to God, "My Delight is in Her," "Married." The new names give intimate and personal expression to the theological reality. (This is even clearer in the Hebrew, since the new names given to Jerusalem by God were indeed used as personal names.)

The image of Jerusalem as a crown of beauty needs to be read in conjunction with Isa. 28:1-6. In that text, after an oracle describing Samaria's doom as what befalls a faded garland (28:1-4), a promise of restoration is included. That promise uses the same language as in 62:3, but in Isa. 28:5-6 God will be the "diadem of beauty" to the remnant of God's people. In Isa. 62:3, what was once promised of God is now extended to God's people. Reading Isa. 62:3 alongside Isa. 28:5-6 also helps the interpreter to see that beauty is not simply an aesthetic category, but derives from the presence of God and God's justice (Isa. 28:6), and as such is a visible sign of salvation.

The third image of restoration, marriage, concludes the lesson. God's joy in Jerusalem is compared to a bridegroom's joy in his bride. The marriage metaphor is a compelling metaphor for restored relationship because it is a metaphor of community, of community formation and communal joy. This is different from the way marriage is often interpreted in the twentieth century, that is, as a private relationship between two individuals. Whenever the marriage metaphor is applied to God in the Old Testament, it is always a metaphor of God and the community. (The language of this metaphor does reflect the marriage customs of ancient Israel, in which the male bridegroom occupied the position of authority in the marital relationship. The preacher, therefore, must be careful about sliding too quickly from the sixth to the twentieth century in opening up this metaphor to the contemporary setting.)

SECOND LESSON: 1 CORINTHIANS 12:1-11

Since lessons from 1 Corinthians 12–15 provide the epistle lessons for the Second through Eighth Sundays after the Epiphany, it is useful to provide a general orientation to 1 Corinthians as a background to the individual Sundays. Paul wrote 1 Corinthians in response to communication he received from and/or about the Corinthian community, and the letter divides into two parts according to the type of information to which Paul is responding. 1 Corinthians 1–6 is Paul's response to news he heard about the Corinthians (cf. 1:11; 3:1; 6:1); 1 Corinthians 7–16 is Paul's response to correspondence the Corinthians have sent to him and questions they have raised. Their concerns include marriage and sex (chap. 7), the relationship between Christians and non-Christians (chaps. 8–10), problems in worship (chaps. 11–14), the resurrection (chap. 15), and the collection of money for churches in need (chap. 16).

The lesson for this Sunday, 1 Cor. 12:1-11, belongs to Paul's responses about worship and is the beginning of his discussion of spiritual gifts. The expression, "now concerning," with which 12:1 begins, suggests that Paul is responding to a community inquiry (cf. 7:1; 8:1). Earlier verses in the letter have suggested that the community was divided over the function and relative value of a wide array of spiritual gifts (1:5-8; 4:7). Verses 2-3 suggest that the community struggled with how one was able to test the Spirit. That is, was ecstatic experience in and of itself proof of the presence of the Spirit? Was there a difference between pagan religious ecstasy and Christian religious ecstasy (v. 2)? In v. 3 Paul clearly establishes the difference between the two. The test for the presence of the Spirit is the content of the ecstatic expression, not simply the fact of ecstatic experience. The only valid spiritual experience is one that is marked by christological confession. Any other confession (including the hyperbolic example, "Let Jesus be cursed") does not derive from the Spirit.

It is important to note that Paul begins his discussion of spiritual gifts with the assumption that there are indeed valid spiritual gifts and ecstatic experiences. He does not argue for or against those experiences, but accepts them as a reality for the Corinthian Christians' worship experience. Contemporary Christians often get caught up in arguing the pros and cons of spiritual gifts, but that is not Paul's argument. Paul accepts the phenomenon as present in the church and moves on to help the Corinthians interpret it theologically.

Verses 4-6 are some of the most eloquent and elegant lines in all of Paul's writings, their eloquence enhanced by their simplicity. Paul begins his discussion of the variety (literally, "distribution") of spiritual gifts with an affirmation of the good news. There are varieties of gifts, services, and activities, but one Spirit, Lord, and God. Paul crafts his affirmation of spiritual diversity to highlight its trinitarian grounding. Whatever the differences in their manifestations, all gifts come from the same source. And all gifts point to the same goal, the common good (v. 7). In a few short phrases, Paul has laid to rest any grounds for squabbling about differences in spiritual gifts. There are different spiritual empowerments, but they come from the same source for the common good.

In vv. 8-10 Paul inventories some of the varieties of spiritual expression. These verses create a vivid picture of the richness of the religious life of the Corinthian community. Paul does not establish a hierarchy among these gifts; he simply lists them as riches of the community (cf. 1:5, 7).

Paul concludes in v. 11 with a reminder that the distribution of the gifts among the community members is completely the Spirit's choosing. This means that the gifts are beyond human control and manipulation. How can one rate different spiritual gifts, value one above another, value the people who hold some gifts more than others, when the gifts come at the Spirit's choosing, and their activation, their work in the community, is the Spirit's work? Spiritual gifts are exactly that—gifts—the presence of God's grace free and at work in the Christian community.

Paul's pastoral and theological acumen is in evidence in this lesson and provides a model for contemporary church leaders. He turns what was a divisive topic for the community into a celebration of God and God's presence in the community through the Spirit.

Third Sunday after the Epiphany

Lutheran	Roman Catholic	Episcopal	Revised Common
Isa. 61:1-6	Neh. 8:2-4a, 5-6, 8-10	Neh. 8:2-10	Neh. 8:1-3, 5-6, 8-10
1 Cor. 12:12-21, 26-27	1 Cor. 12:12-30 or 1 Cor. 12:12-14, 27	1 Cor. 12:12-27	1 Cor. 12:12-31a
Luke 4:14-21	Luke 1:1-4; 4:14-21	Luke 4:14-21	Luke 4:14-21

The lessons from Luke and Nehemiah complement one another; they both depict scenes of the public reading and interpretation of Scripture. Together they offer the preacher a fresh vantage point from which to explore the role of proclamation in the life of the community. This lesson from Luke begins the semi-continuous reading of Luke as the Gospel lesson throughout ordinary time in this lectionary cycle. (The Roman Catholic Lectionary's inclusion of Luke 1:1-4 marks the beginning of this Lukan cycle.) The epistle lesson continues the readings from 1 Corinthians 12–15.

FIRST LESSON: NEHEMIAH 8:1-10

The books of Ezra and Nehemiah contain a narrative account of the restoration of Jerusalem after the Babylonian exile. The poetry of Isaiah 60–62, the Old Testament lessons for prior Sundays after the Epiphany (and the Lutheran lesson for this Sunday) comes from an earlier stage of the restoration, closer to Cyrus's edict of 538 B.C.E. that permitted Jerusalem to be rebuilt, whereas Ezra and Nehemiah reflect the restoration work of the fifth and fourth centuries B.C.E. The primary focus of the books of Ezra and Nehemiah is on the religious restoration of Jerusalem. It was not enough to rebuild the city and the temple; the religious life of the community also had to be rebuilt according to the law of Moses. The particular lesson for this Sunday, Neh. 8:1-10, seems to have been dislodged from its original location during the transmission of the text, because it belongs to the story of Ezra, not Nehemiah. (The reference to Nehemiah in 8:9 is probably a scribal addition to integrate the Ezra story into its current location in Nehemiah.)

Nehemiah 8:1-10 narrates a story of Ezra's public reading of the law of Moses. The story is not hard to follow: The people gather in the public square to listen to Ezra read the law; the law is read and its interpretation given. The significance of the story lies in its unfolding of the interrelationship of the people, the book of the law, and the interpreter of the law. (The interpretation of Neh. 8:1-10 that follows owes much to the insights of Gene M. Tucker, "Reading and Preaching the Old Testament," in *Listening to the Word: Studies in Honor of Fred B. Craddock*, ed. by Gail R. O'Day and Thomas G. Long [Nashville: Abingdon Press, 1993].)

Verse 1 identifies "all the people" as the group who call for the public reading of the law. The public meeting thus is not called by the religious professionals but by the people themselves. The lesson is punctuated by references to the gathered assembly (vv. 1, 2, 3, 5, 6, 7, 8, 9), and those references make clear that the law is the people's book. The people want to know what the law says to them.

References to "the book of the law" also punctuate the lesson. The story is told in a way that highlights the book's presence: the book is asked for (v. 1); the book of the law is brought before the assembly (v. 2); Ezra opens "the book in the sight of all the people, for he was standing above all the people" (v. 5). The gathering around the law is not simply oral/aural; that is, it is not simply speaking and hearing. It also involves *seeing*. The book of the law is not the scribe's private possession, hidden away so that the assembly only has the interpreter's word. Rather, the written text itself is visible and available to all. The physical presence of the book is another way of showing that the law is the people's book.

The priest and scribe Ezra (along with his associates, vv. 4, 7) is thus positioned in the story as the bridge between the people and their book. He is at the same time the servant of the people and the servant of the book. The people need the scribe's assistance in interpreting what the book says. To begin with, the book of the law was written in Hebrew and Jews at the time of Ezra spoke Aramaic. Part of the interpreter's task therefore involved translation. But scribal interpretation involved more than translation; the scribes also assisted in opening up the meaning of the text (v. 8). The people needed the scribes, those trained in the study of the law, so that the fullness of the law might be available to them.

The interrelationship of book, people, and law receives its fullest expression in vv. 9-10. The reading of the law initially causes the people to weep, perhaps out of awe, the inscrutable presence of the holy, or a need for repentance. But the interpreter Ezra reminds the people that the reading of the law is not an occasion for mourning, but celebration. The law is God's gift to God's people (cf. Deut. 5:1-5, 31-33; 12:1). As God's gift, the law brings strength to the people, and their strength is God's joy (v. 10). The public proclamation of the law and its interpretation is an occasion of joy because it reminds the people of who their God is, what their God makes available to them for life, and who they can be if they live in the joy of God's word (e.g., ". . . send portions of [food] to those for whom nothing is prepared," v. 10). The people knew they needed to hear God's word. That is why they summoned the scribe to bring the law to them. This lesson is a reminder that it is the scribe's responsibility (and joy) to meet the people's need and assist in making the written word of God available and alive in the gathered community.

GOSPEL: LUKE 4:14-21

The Gospel lessons for the Third and Fourth Sundays after the Epiphany, Luke 4:14-21 and 4:21-30 (32), are really one textual unit divided into two parts for expediency. Together the two lessons constitute Jesus' "Nazareth inaugural," Jesus' preaching in his home synagogue that functions in Luke as the inauguration of Jesus' public ministry (cf. the placement of the story in Matt. 13:54-58 and Mark 6:1-6). When the text is read according to the lectionary divisions, vv. 16-21 reads as a story of prophetic fulfillment, vv. 21-30 as a story of prophetic rejection. It is important for the lectionary preacher to remember that the two Sundays must be interpreted together.

Luke 4:16-21 provides an important glimpse into synagogue worship at the time of Jesus and into Jesus' religious life. Luke 4:16 says that it was Jesus' custom to go to the synagogue on the Sabbath, a reminder that Jesus was an observant Jew (see also 2:21, 22, 41-42). Any male belonging to the synagogue community could be invited by the synagogue president to read the lesson for the day and give words of interpretation, and this is the role given to Jesus in this text. The synagogue service consisted of a recitation of a psalm, readings from the Law and the Prophets, a sermon based on the day's Scripture, and a benediction. The early Christians adopted this order of service for their worship and added the celebration of the Eucharist to it. Christian worship today thus continues in the tradition of synagogue worship, and Christian preaching as the exposition of Scripture traces its roots to synagogue preaching.

The picture of synagogue worship in Luke 4:16-21 is quite detailed. Luke narrates the story with a kind of "you were there" realism. He paints the scene so that the Gospel reader is positioned as a member of the synagogue congregation: watching Jesus stand up to read (v. 16), seeing the Isaiah scroll handed to Jesus, watching Jesus unroll the scroll, find the text (v. 17), read the text (vv. 18-19), roll up the scroll and hand it to the attendant, then sit down (v. 20). When Luke writes, "The eyes of all in the synagogue were fixed upon him" (v. 20), the reader is one of those pair of eyes, because the reader has seen exactly what the synagogue audience in the story saw.

The center of the story is Jesus' reading from Isaiah in 4:18-19. The Scripture quotation in those verses is a conflation of Isa. 61:1-2 and 58:6. Isaiah 61 (the Lutheran Old Testament lesson) celebrates the prophet's vocation as the one who speaks consolation to Jerusalem as it faces the work of restoration after exile. The prophet proclaims the end of the suffering and despair of exile and the beginning of freedom and new life. Isaiah 61:1 acknowledges the prophet's vocation as something for which he has been chosen by God, anointed by the Spirit.

The words about anointing have particular significance. At Jesus' baptism he was anointed with the Holy Spirit (3:21), but God's announcement of the anointing was spoken to Jesus alone ("You are my Son, the Beloved; with you I am well pleased," 3:22). Now, in the presence of the gathered assembly in the Nazareth synagogue, Jesus makes the public announcement of that anointing and states its purpose. He is the anointed messenger of the good news to the poor, the captives, the blind, the oppressed. He is the preacher of liberation, of the new social reality.

Jesus begins his exposition of the text with a dramatic pronouncement, "Today this scripture has been fulfilled in your hearing" (v. 21). The promises of Isaiah 61 have their fulfillment in Jesus; the promised time of consolation and comfort is now under way. This is a bold claim and a bold beginning for Jesus' ministry. Everything that follows in Jesus' ministry in Luke can be seen and heard as the enactment of God's promises of freedom made in Isaiah 61. There is no mystery about the vocation of Luke's Jesus: He is the fulfillment of God's promised liberation. And because of the way Luke has told the story, placing the reader as a member of the synagogue congregation, the fulfillment of the promises extends beyond the Gospel story to include any Christian community that reads this Scripture.

Most preachers would not consider boldly announcing, "Today this scripture has been fulfilled in your hearing," but in many ways that claim is implicit in every sermon as the preacher seeks to make the word of God a reality for those who listen. The fulfillment of Isaiah 61 in Jesus is a singular event, but the belief that the promises of Scripture can be realized *today* in the hearing of the worshiping community is not limited to that event. Rather, the fulfillment of God's promises in Jesus invites the church to live as if the promises of God will be fulfilled in its hearing today and for todays to come.

SECOND LESSON: 1 CORINTHIANS 12:12-31a

The epistle lesson (1 Cor. 12:12-31a) is Paul's metaphor of the church as the body of Christ, one of the most well-known passages in Paul, indeed, perhaps in all the New Testament. In 1 Cor. 12:12-13 Paul establishes the foundational metaphor. He moves from the anatomical example ("For just as the body . . .") to his christological and ecclesiological claim ("so it is with Christ," v. 12). It is important to note that Paul does not move from the anatomical image to a comment about the *church* as body, but to *Christ* as body. That is because, as v. 13 makes clear, it is the oneness of Christ that forms disparate members into one body. This is a significant theological distinction that is sometimes lost in popular appropriation of Paul's metaphor. It is not that the church is literally the body of Christ, as if the members of the church together constitute the body of Christ. Rather, because each Christian is one with Christ, together they form a body, the church. Paul points to baptism (v. 13), each Christian's dying and rising with Christ (Rom. 6:3-5; Gal. 3:27) as what makes it possible for diverse social (slave, free) and ethnic groups (Jew, Greek) to become one body. The number "one" occurs five times in vv. 12-13 and emphasizes the foundational unity to which Paul makes appeal.

Paul's elaboration of the body metaphor can be divided into three parts: vv. 14-21, in which Paul uses vivid, playful body imagery; vv. 22-26, in which Paul moves away from the vivid imagery to a metaphor built around social relationships; and vv. 27-31a, in which Paul directly discusses the church as the body of Christ.

Verses 14-21 need little commentary, because their images speak eloquently for themselves. Paul paints a wonderful picture of the mutuality of body parts that enables a body to function as a whole. The talking foot and ear of vv. 15-16 show the absurdity of one body part feeling excluded because it is not the same as another member. The image of the body consisting of only one sense organ (v. 17) communicates a similar sense of the absurdity of desiring the exclusive presence of any one body part. Verse 18 acknowledges God as the author of the diversity of the body (cf. 1 Cor. 12:4-6). The talking eye and head of v. 21 highlight the absurdity of one member desiring to eliminate another. Paul never breaks out of the metaphor in these verses; he does not turn didactic or hortatory. He raises questions to help the Corinthians see the absurdity of trying to privilege one member of the body over another, but he never tells them what to do. Instead he allows the vivid images to speak for themselves.

In vv. 22-26 Paul breaks out of the body images somewhat to address some of the causes of dissension within the Corinthian community (v. 25).

He still refrains from didacticisms, but the pictures he paints of the body in these verses derive more from the Corinthians' experience than they do from anatomy. The language about mutuality in respect and honor (vv. 22-25), suffering and rejoicing (v. 26) points to the ways the Christian community as body should function. In 1 Corinthians 8–10, Paul has already addressed the theme of weaker members (8:7-13; 10:27-29) and he returns to that theme here. The Corinthians are not treating one another the way members of a body need to treat one another in order to function together as one body and not disintegrate into individual members.

In vv. 27-31a Paul begins with a restatement of vv. 12-13 (the church is the body of Christ) and then leaves body imagery behind in order to address directly the wide array of "members"—gifts—that form the Corinthian body of Christ. Paul singles out apostles, prophets, and teachers (v. 28a), ministers of the word, because their ministries were the foundational ministries out of which the community grew. Paul then lists other gifts (v. 28b; cf. 12:8-10) and goes on to ask, as he did for eyes and ears, Can all be one thing? Just as it is absurd to conceive of a human body made up solely of eyes, it is also absurd to think of the body of Christ where all have the same gift. A body needs individual members in order to be a body. Members should not be excluded because their gifts appear to be less valuable. Paul established the criterion for determining the value of spiritual gifts in 12:7, that they work for the common good, and he urges the Corinthians toward the goal in v. 31a. The "greater gifts" are those that build up the community (cf. 10:23).

In contemporary ecumenical conversations, discussion of the church as the body of Christ is usually framed in terms of how the church can act so as to become the one body of Christ. This approach turns Paul's metaphor inside out, however, and diminishes its ecclesiological power. Paul begins with the affirmation that the church *is* the one body of Christ, and then examines the significance of that unity for the Christian community's actions. The church universal should listen carefully to Paul's body language.

Fourth Sunday after the Epiphany

Lutheran	Roman Catholic	Episcopal	Revised Common
Jer. 1:4-10	Jer. 1:4-5, 17-19	Jer. 1:4-10	Jer. 1:4-10
1 Cor. 12:27—13:13	1 Cor. 12:31—13:13 or 1 Cor. 13:4-13	1 Cor. 14:12b-20	1 Cor. 13:1-13
Luke 4:21-32	Luke 4:21-30	Luke 4:21-32	Luke 4:21-30

The Gospel lesson concludes the story of Jesus in the Nazareth synagogue (for the first half of this story, see the Third Sunday after the Epiphany). The Old Testament lesson is the call and commission of the prophet Jeremiah. This lesson helps to place Jesus' ministry in the broader story of the careers of Israel's prophets. The epistle lesson continues the readings from 1 Corinthians 12–15.

GOSPEL: LUKE 4:21-32

The lectionary divides Luke 4:16-30 so that Luke 4:21 appears on both the Third and Fourth Sundays after the Epiphany. On the Third Sunday, Luke 4:21 is used as a formula of fulfillment and conclusion; it looks back to Jesus' reading of Isaiah 61 and reflects on its fulfillment in Jesus. On the Fourth Sunday, Luke 4:21 becomes a formula of beginning and an anticipatory announcement. It looks forward to 4:22-30 as the fulfillment.

The initial response of the synagogue crowd to Jesus' words and presence is positive. They are amazed and pleased by their hometown boy ("Is not this Joseph's son?"). The "gracious words" (v. 22) are the words of Scripture that he read and his announcement of their fulfillment; Jesus has been impressive in his role as synagogue lector. It is when Jesus assumes the role of the interpreter of Scripture, the synagogue preacher, that his relationship to the home crowd shifts.

Jesus' sermon is in two parts: v. 23 and vv. 24-27. Both parts are organized around a proverb that Jesus quotes. The proverb in v. 23*a*, "Doctor, cure yourself," was common in ancient literature, appearing in both Greek and rabbinical literature. Jesus' use of the proverb here has a harsh turn to it, because it challenges the crowd's perception of Jesus and the expectations they place on him. Verse 23*b* makes this challenge clear: Jesus criticizes the hometown crowd for their desire for signs, but also for their desire that he do for his own what they have heard he has done for outsiders.

Verses 24-27 expand on the conflict between insider and outsider. Jesus quotes another proverb ("no prophet is accepted in the prophet's hometown") that explicitly addresses the question of the prophet's relationship to his own. This proverb occurs as part of Jesus' teaching in all four Gospels (Mark 6:4; Matt. 13:57; John 4:44) as well as in noncanonical documents (the Gospel of Thomas and Oxyrhynchus Papyri). It addresses one of the central themes of Jesus' ministry in Luke: the pattern of acceptance and rejection in response to Jesus' words and works and the redefinition of Jesus' "own" as a result of people's response (cf. 2:34-35). To be from Jesus' home does not mean that one has a special claim on him.

In vv. 25-27 Jesus illustrates that prophetic ministry is not limited by hometown boundaries by reminding the crowd of two events in the ministries of Elijah and Elisha. In vv. 25-26 Jesus alludes to the story of Elijah and the widow of Sidon (1 Kings 17:1, 8-24). God sent Elijah to the widow during the famine, and from the bare essentials of her larder, God enabled Elijah to bring forth a miraculous supply of food that sustained the household (1 Kings 17:8-16). Elijah is also portrayed as bringing the woman's critically ill son back to life (1 Kings 17:17-24). Both miracles are performed for a foreigner. In v. 27 Jesus reminds the synagogue audience of Elisha's cleansing of Namaan (2 Kings 5:1-19). Namaan was a foreign warrior who was brought to Elisha for healing of leprosy. Namaan accepts Elisha's command that he wash in the waters of the Jordan (even though Namaan protests that the rivers of Damascus are superior to those of Israel, vv. 10-12), is healed, and worships the God of Israel (vv. 13-16).

Jesus uses both stories to show that God's gift of life is not limited to Israel, but is available to the nations (non-Israelites) as well. In the context of Jesus' own ministry and the immediate setting in the Nazareth synagogue, Jesus is telling the hometown crowd that the ministry for which he was anointed (4:18-19) is not limited to Israel, but like the work of Elijah and Elisha, includes the nations. The vision of social transformation that Isaiah 61 announces is a universal, not parochial vision. The fulfillment of which Jesus speaks in 4:21 moves beyond Israel's borders.

It is Jesus' announcement of the universality of God's promises that turns the crowd against him. The contrast between v. 23 and vv. 28-29 is staggering as the crowd's reaction turns from adulation to murderous rage. Jesus escapes unharmed (v. 30), but the power of the crowd's rejection lingers. When Jesus challenged them with the radical universality of his mission, with the radical inclusivity of the good news, his own rejected him. Their privileged status as God's chosen people was threatened by Jesus' opening of his ministry to "outsiders." This tension between insiders and outsiders in the gospel is an issue with which the contemporary church continues to struggle.

(Luke 4:31-32 are the introduction to the next pericope, Jesus in the synagogue in Capernaum [4:31-37], but the Lutheran and Episcopal lectionaries position them as the conclusion to this lesson. While removing these two verses from the Capernaum story ignores the literary integrity of 4:31-37, their inclusion with this lesson provides a glimpse of how Jesus' ministry continued after Nazareth. Jesus was not stopped by the reaction in his hometown, but instead enacted what he had taught in vv. 23-27. He went from his "hometown" of Judea to the "outsiders" in Galilee.)

FIRST LESSON: JEREMIAH 1:4-10

The conflict in Luke 4:21-30 arises when Jesus' prophetic vocation, so boldly announced in 4:18-19, is interpreted as including the nations in its promises. In Jer. 1:4-10 Jeremiah is explicitly positioned as prophet to the nations from the beginning of his ministry.

Jeremiah 1:4-10 is the call and commission of the prophet Jeremiah. Jeremiah's ministry took place at the end of the seventh century, in the years leading up to the Babylonian exile of 587 B.C.E. (1:1-3). During Jeremiah's ministry, the kings of Judah were engaged in a dangerous political game of trying to appease both the Babylonian and Egyptian empires in order to preserve Judah's political sovereignty. In the end, Judah lost its sovereignty to Babylon. Jeremiah's prophetic ministry attempted to engage the political realities of Judah's struggles in theological categories. The call and commission of 1:4-10 highlight the union of the political and theological in Jeremiah's ministry.

Jeremiah 1:4-10 contains elements of prophetic call and commission common to other Old Testament call narratives. The standard elements include:

God's initiative	vv. 4-5
The prophet's resistance	v. 6
God's rebuke and reassurance	vv. 7-8
Physical act of commissioning	v. 9a
The content of the commission	vv. 9b-10

God's initiative in calling Jeremiah is expressed in v. 4 as "the word of the Lord" coming to him. The expression "word of the Lord" occurs regularly in Jeremiah to underscore that Jeremiah's words are in reality God's word. The particular shape of God's initiative is expressed in v. 5. God had a plan and purpose for Jeremiah that antedates Jeremiah's conception ("before

I formed you in the womb"). The parallelism of the two temporal clauses ("before . . . before") shows that everything about Jeremiah belongs to God's plan. The verbs used to describe God's intentions are significant: knew, consecrated, appointed. There can be no question that this is God's initiative.

The vocation to which God appoints Jeremiah is also significant: to be a prophet to the nations (v. 5). The nations include Babylon, Egypt, Assyria, and Judah itself. Jeremiah is not called to a parochial vocation, to be enacted within the confines of the Jerusalem temple or even God's covenant people. Jeremiah is called to make God known on the global stage.

Jeremiah's protest in v. 6 (cf. Exod. 4:10) focuses on his inexperience and inability to speak. His protest is immediately rebuked by God (v. 7). Jeremiah's inexperience is irrelevant because God sends him, and his inability to speak is irrelevant because God tells him what to say. God does not greet Jeremiah's fears only with a rebuke, however. In v. 8 God speaks words of reassurance, bolstering Jeremiah with a reminder that God is with him. (Verses 17-19, additional verses included in the Roman Catholic lectionary, are a metaphorical restatement of God's words of reassurance in vv. 7-8.)

Verse 9a is the symbolic enactment of Jeremiah's commission: God touches his mouth (cf. 15:16; Isa. 6:6-7). In v. 9b God interprets the symbolism. With God's word in Jeremiah's mouth, God then gives Jeremiah the substance of his commission (v. 10).

Jeremiah's appointment as prophet to the nations is repeated in v. 10, and the significance of this repetition should not be overlooked. Nations and kingdoms are competing for Judah's attention, and they are all competing for their place on the world political scene. Jeremiah is appointed to put God's word solidly and inescapably into the mix. The history of nations and kingdoms will not be determined separately from God's sovereign word. God's prophet does not simply have a "religious" vocation; God's prophet has a vocation that draws the prophet into all aspects and spheres of human life.

Jeremiah's commission is expressed metaphorically in three pairs of verbs, two negative pairs ("to pluck up and pull down," "to destroy and to overthrow"), one positive pair ("to build and to plant"). These pairs of verbs introduce motifs that recur throughout the book of Jeremiah to express the heart of Jeremiah's ministry (see 12:14-15, 17; 18:7-10; 31:28; 42:10; 45:4). His prophetic ministry will involve the deconstruction of existing structures and realities, and indeed, that negative activity will be the heart of his vocation (note the weighting of the verb pairs toward the negative). But Jeremiah's ministry also contains the promise of newness: building will follow the pulling down; planting will follow the plucking up. Verse 10 is a clear statement that Jeremiah's ministry will be conflictual and costly, but that newness may arise from that very conflict and cost.

SECOND LESSON: 1 CORINTHIANS 12:27—13:13

1 Corinthians 12:31—13:13 provides a theologically rich counterpoint to the images of prophetic rejection and vocational risk in the lessons from Luke and Jeremiah. This lyrical chapter on love does indeed trace "the more excellent way" with its vision of community love that embodies the love of God.

1 Corinthians 13:1-13 divides into three parts: vv. 1-3, 4-7, 8-13. In vv. 1-3 Paul contrasts the spiritual gifts and religious behaviors held in esteem by the Corinthian community with love. Each of the gifts that Paul cites may be valuable in the life of the community—speaking in tongues (v. 1), prophecy, wisdom, faith (v. 2), almsgiving and handing over one's body (perhaps implying martyrdom, v. 3)—but even these valuable gifts are nothing if love does not drive them. Love is the only thing that can determine the value of spiritual gifts. Having shown the necessity of love in the community's use of its gifts, Paul then goes on to describe what love is (vv. 4-7). His description of love is both positive (vv. 4a, 6b-7) and negative (vv. 4b-6a). The picture that Paul paints of love is the opposite of the picture that has emerged of the Corinthian community throughout the epistle—quarrelsome, self-consumed, arrogant, intolerant of differences. When one looks at the Corinthians' conduct, one might be led to assume that the very love of which Paul speaks is absent. Paul paints a picture of love that leads human community out of base hurtfulness into a community of patience, kindness, rejoicing, faith, and hope.

In the concluding section, vv. 8-13, Paul returns to the contrast between love and other spiritual gifts. His contrast is built around his assertion in v. 8, "love never ends," and thus is based on the eschatological reality of love. Human achievement and accomplishment, even the most valued and valuable spiritual gifts (prophecy, tongues, knowledge, vv. 8-9) are fleeting and partial, but love endures and transcends human mutability. In vv. 8-13 the line between the human expression of love and God as love blurs, because Paul's words make it clear that love itself is God's gift to us, indeed is God's greatest gift (v. 13).

The key to understanding Paul's view of love comes in v. 12: "Now I know only in part; then I will know fully, even as I have been fully known." Humans have received the wonderful gift of being known by God (cf. 8:3). God's full knowledge of humanity is the beginning point of all God's gifts, and with each gift humans participate in God's knowledge and love. God's three great enduring gifts are faith, hope, and love (v. 13). The "greatest of these is love" because God is love. That is, in God's gift of love, God gives human beings their fullest share in the character of God. Paul is right to say that "love never ends," because love is the beginning and the ending. Love is God.

Christians are most familiar with this rich text from 1 Corinthians 13 as a standard text at weddings. Because of this common usage, the church must be careful lest it reduce this text to a celebration of human love, and in particular, the love between two individuals. This text celebrates the love between two individuals only insofar as that love is one expression of the love that gives life and shape to the larger Christian community. And this text celebrates the love that should be at the heart of Christian community only insofar as that love is recognized as the presence of God and God's love in the community. This eloquent, inspiring text celebrates what is possible in human community because of who God is and what God does.

EPISCOPAL SECOND LESSON: 1 CORINTHIANS 14:12b-20

The Episcopal Lectionary skips 1 Corinthians 13 and moves ahead to Paul's discussion of spiritual gifts in 14:12b-20. In these verses Paul continues to move the Corinthian community toward understanding communal edification, "the building up of the church" (v. 12), as the goal of all gifts. To that end, in vv. 13-19 Paul stresses the importance of spirit and intellect in worship. The intellect is needed so that one person's individual spiritual experience can be deprivatized and made accessible and comprehensible to the whole community.

Fifth Sunday after the Epiphany

Lutheran	Roman Catholic	Episcopal	Revised Common
Isa. 6:1-8 (9-13)	Isa. 6:1-2a, 3-8	Judg. 6:11-24a	Isa. 6:1-8 (9-13)
1 Cor. 14:12b-20	1 Cor. 15:1-11 *or* 1 Cor. 15:3-8, 11	1 Cor. 15:1-11	1 Cor. 15:1-11
Luke 5:1-11	Luke 5:1-11	Luke 5:1-11	Luke 5:1-11

The Old Testament lesson for this Sunday is another call narrative (cf. Jer. 1:4-10, the Fourth Sunday after the Epiphany), but the homiletical focus of the call narrative is different from the preceding Sunday because of its pairing with the Gospel lesson, Jesus' gathering of his first disciples. This Sunday's combination of Old Testament and Gospel lessons focuses on the vocation of discipleship. The epistle lesson continues the readings from 1 Corinthians 12–15.

FIRST LESSON: ISAIAH 6:1-8

Isaiah 6:1-8 narrates the call of the prophet Isaiah. Verses 1-4 describe Isaiah's vision, v. 5 describes the prophet's response to the vision, and vv. 6-8 describe the cleansing and call of the prophet. (Verses 9-13, optional additional verses in the Lutheran and Revised Common Lectionaries, contain the substance of Isaiah's commission.)

Verse 1 provides a chronological referent for the beginning of Isaiah's prophetic ministry, "in the year that King Uzziah died" (742 B.C.E.). Prophetic call narratives frequently open by grounding the prophet's call in contemporary history (e.g., Jer. 1:1-3; Hos. 1:1; Amos 1:1; cf. Luke 3:1). What is striking about v. 1a is the combination of concrete historical grounding with an extrasensory vision (cf. Ezek. 1:1-3). The prophet's vision will take him outside ordinary experience, but the reader is reminded that the prophet is nonetheless located in this world.

The prophet's experience is both visionary and auditory: he sees (vv. 1, 2, 4) and hears (v. 3). What Isaiah sees is God seated on a throne within the temple, surrounded by heavenly creatures. That God's greatness is beyond human reckoning is conveyed by the details of the vision in v. 1: a high and lofty throne, the hem of the robe that fills the temple. That God's presence is beyond human description is also conveyed by v. 1, because the prophet does not describe God directly, but only the signs of greatness that surround God.

The description of the seraphs contributes to the sense of awe in the presence of God. The seraphs cover their faces, suggesting the heavenly host, like human beings, cannot look directly on the face of God (cf. Exod. 33:20). "Feet" is a euphemism in the Old Testament for genitals (Exod. 4:25; Isa. 7:20); the seraphs are thus depicted like Adam and Eve, hiding their nakedness before God (Gen. 3:7, 10-11). Even heavenly creatures are in awe of God.

In v. 3 the seraphs announce God's holiness to one another. The threefold "holy, holy, holy" emphasizes God's wholly otherness and is the fullest expression of God's divinity. Verse 3*b* moves the praise of God in a slightly different direction; even though God's holiness renders God wholly other, the earth bears testimony to God's presence ("glory"; cf. Ps. 19:1). God is both beyond human experience and present in human experience. When the church sings the words of Isa. 6:3 in the Sanctus of the eucharistic liturgy, it adds its voice to the seraphs' hymn of praise. The shaking of the temple (v. 4*a*) shows that even the site of the Holy of Holies is affected by the presence and praise of God. The smoke (v. 4*b*) is further indication of God's presence, because smoke was a frequent accompaniment of theophanies in the Old Testament (e.g., Exod. 19:9, 18; 24:15ff.).

Isaiah's experience of the presence of God reminds him of human failings before God (v. 5). His confession of uncleanness acknowledges that failing and the distance it creates between God and humanity. His words begin with a statement of awe, because Hebrew tradition taught that a person could not look on the face of God and live (e.g., Exod. 33:20; 19:21; Judg. 6:22). Isaiah assumes his death is imminent, because he, a mere mortal, has seen God.

Instead of death, however, Isaiah receives a staggering gift of God's grace (vv. 6-8). God forgives Isaiah's sinfulness. This forgiveness is enacted in two ways. First, in vv. 6-7*a*, one of the seraphs enacts a ritual cleansing through the purification of fire. Second, in v. 7*b*, the seraph recites a formula of forgiveness and absolution. Through ritual word and deed, Isaiah receives God's grace.

As a recipient of God's gracious forgiveness, Isaiah no longer encounters God in terror (cf. v. 5) but in joyful readiness. When the voice of God inquires after a messenger (note that instead of an explicit call there is a question), Isaiah volunteers himself for God's service. He offers himself in response to the gift that he has received from God. The beginning of Isaiah's ministry is thus depicted as a drama of human response to the holiness and graciousness of God.

FIFTH SUNDAY AFTER THE EPIPHANY

EPISCOPAL FIRST LESSON: JUDGES 6:11-24*a*

Judges 6:11-24*a*, the Old Testament lesson in the Episcopal Lectionary, is also a call narrative, the call of Gideon. It contains many of the standard elements of the prophetic call narratives (cf. Jer. 1:4-10): theophany (v. 12), protest (vv. 13, 15, 22), commissioning (v. 14), words of reassurance (vv. 16, 18, 23). The story of Gideon is a long call narrative, because it incorporates Gideon's request for a sign (v. 17) and the enactment of the sign (vv. 19-21). Like the Isaiah 6 narrative, Gideon's call involves a theophany that leaves him in terror for his life (v. 22). And like the Isaiah narrative, Gideon's terror is met by the gracious, peace-filled presence of God (vv. 23-24).

GOSPEL: LUKE 5:1-11

Luke 5:1-11, like Isa. 6:1-8, narrates an event in which an experience of the presence of God leads to the embrace of a new vocation. A variety of Jesus traditions are brought together by Luke to form this story: Jesus' teaching in a boat (vv. 1-3; cf. Mark 4:1-2), the unexpected catch of fish (vv. 4-10*a*; cf. John 21:1-11), the call of Simon and the first disciples (vv. 10*b*-11; cf. Mark 1:16-20).

Jesus' seaside teaching in vv. 1-3 is the first instance of Jesus' teaching outside a synagogue in Luke (cf. 4:15; 16-30; 31-37; 43-44). The mention of the crowd and its behavior in v. 1 suggests the growing success and appeal of Jesus' ministry; the crowd's desire to hear "the word of God" cannot be satisfied by synagogue meetings. They come to Jesus, not waiting for him to come to them. The fishermen and their two boats (v. 2) provide a vivid tableau of first-century Palestinian fishing practices. The mention of Simon in v. 3, however, suggests that the fishermen are more than window dressing. This is the second mention of Simon in Luke. In Luke 4:38-39 Jesus was a guest at Simon's house and healed Simon's mother-in-law of a fever. Unlike the call of Simon in Mark (1:16-20) and Matthew (4:18-22), which is the first meeting of Jesus and Simon, in Luke Simon has previous knowledge of Jesus and his miraculous powers.

In vv. 4-10*a* the focus shifts from a teaching story to a miracle story. In rough form these verses contain the standard elements of a miracle story: a situation of lack (no fish, v. 5); the miracle (the unexpected catch, vv. 6-7); response to and attestation of the miracle (vv. 8-10*a*).

After Jesus finishes teaching, he gives Simon two commands about fishing (v. 4, "put out," "let down"). As is typical of Simon's response to Jesus' words in all four Gospels (e.g., Matt. 14:28-30; Mark 8:31-33; John 13:8-10), Simon begins by measuring Jesus' words against his own assessment of the situation. As is also typical of Simon, however, he does not allow his initial assessment to have the decisive say. Despite his sense of the improbability of catching any fish, Simon trusts Jesus' command. The noun *master* in v. 5 occurs only in Luke among the Gospels and is used in places where the other Synoptic Gospels use "teacher." Its use here suggests that from the moment Jesus requested the use of Simon's boat (v. 3), Simon recognized Jesus as the one in command.

Verses 6-7 narrate the catch of fish. Every detail in these two verses— the strain on the nets (v. 6), the need to summon help (v. 7*a*); the threat of sinking (v. 7*b*)—underscores the magnitude of the catch. This was no ordinary fishing trip!

Simon's response to the catch in v. 8 makes the extraordinariness of the moment theologically explicit. Simon prostrates himself at Jesus' knees and acknowledges him as "Lord" (no longer merely "Master"). Simon thus recognizes the catch of fish as a manifestation of the presence of God in Jesus. Simon's acknowledgment of his sinfulness in response to the miracle has puzzled many commentators. The lectionary juxtaposition of Luke 5:1-10 and Isa. 6:1-8 helps to unravel the mystery. In Isa. 6:5 and Luke 5:8, the experience of the presence of God brings human failings before God into stark relief. Both Isaiah's and Simon's confessions of their unworthiness ("unclean," Isa. 6:5; "sinful," Luke 5:8) acknowledge the distance between God and humanity and human dependence on God's initiative in bridging that distance. Neither Isaiah nor Simon has done anything out of the ordinary to merit God's presence to them. God makes God's self available, in the heavenly vision of Isa. 6:1-8, in the miraculous catch of Luke 5:6-7, because of God's grace, not human accomplishment.

The amazement of "all who were with him" (v. 9, those in Simon's boat) and of James and John (v. 10*a*, presumably the fishermen in the second boat) shows that Simon is not alone in his response to the catch. In v. 10*b* Jesus turns the moment of amazement into one of commission. His words are directed specifically to Simon (the "you" is a second person singular), but the response of all the fishermen in v. 11 shows that they understood themselves to be addressed as well. Jesus' opening words ("Do not be afraid") are a standard part of call and commission narratives (e.g., Jer. 1:8; Judg. 6:23): words of assurance in the face of the awesome presence of God. The substance of the commission is given distinctly Lukan wording: "from now on you will be catching people." The expression "catching people" literally means "you will be capturing people alive." Both Mark 1:17 and Matt. 4:19 use a fishing metaphor here, but Luke's verb is more general and seems to imply that Simon will join Jesus in bringing people from death to life.

In v. 11 Simon and his companions accept Jesus' commission. The totality of their acceptance is conveyed by the notice that "they left everything."

The verb "follow" is frequently used as a metaphor for discipleship in Luke (e.g., 5:27-28; 9:23, 49, 57, 59, 61). The lectionary's juxtaposition of Isa. 6:1-8 and Luke 5:1-11 provides the preacher with two rich pictures of the interrelationship of an encounter with the presence of God and the call into God's service. In both narratives, an experience of God's grace (in the act of purification in Isa. 6:6-7, in the abundant catch of fish in Luke 5:6-7) evokes a full embrace of God's call to service (Isa. 6:8; Luke 5:10b-11). Isaiah and Simon both embrace a vocation of making available to others what they themselves have experienced of God.

SECOND LESSON: 1 CORINTHIANS 15:1-11

(For the Lutheran epistle lesson, 1 Corinthians 14:12b-20, see comments on Episcopal epistle lesson, the Fourth Sunday after the Epiphany.)

In 1 Corinthians 15 Paul engages the Corinthians in a theologically rich discussion of the nature of the resurrection and its significance for Christian faith and life. Paul introduces this discussion in 1 Cor. 15:1-11 with a restatement of the core Gospel he has preached to the Corinthian church. This passage can be divided into three parts: vv. 1-2, introduction; vv. 3-7, recital of the gospel; vv. 8-11, Paul's own experience of the gospel.

It is important to remember that when Paul speaks about the good news (gospel), he is not referring to a written gospel, but to the proclamation of the good news of Jesus. Paul twice refers to his proclamation of the gospel (vv. 1, 2), but the real emphasis in vv. 1-2 is on the Corinthians' responsibility as recipients of the gospel. He describes the Corinthians' relationship to the gospel in a variety of ways: "which . . . you received," "in which you stand," "through which also you are being saved." The good news, the key to the Corinthians' salvation, has been made available to them. If they move away from the gospel that was preached to them, they also move away from their salvation (v. 2).

In vv. 3-7 Paul reminds the Corinthians of that gospel. Verse 3 begins with the language of tradition ("handed over," "received"). Paul did not coin the core proclamation himself, but stands as one witness to the gospel. In these verses Paul thus makes use of early Christian creedal tradition.

Verses 3-5 contain the oldest written testimony to the death and resurrection of Christ. The creed contains two parallel parts that each consists of a main verb, a reference to Scripture, and a corroborating verb (see chart on p. 38). The reference to the burial underscores the reality of the death; the reference to the appearances underscores the reality of the resurrection. In both parts of the creed, the reference to Scripture is general. The creed highlights that Christ's death and resurrection are part of God's plan as revealed in Scripture and does not engage in specific proofs from Scripture. Verses 3-5 contain the core of traditions that lie behind the expanded death and resurrection narratives of the four Gospels.

	Main verb	Scripture	Corroborating verb
Death	died	in accordance with Scripture	was buried
Resurrection	was raised	in accordance with Scripture	appeared

In vv. 6-7 Paul expands the core traditions, mentioning additional appearances of the risen Christ. This expansion serves three purposes. First, it opens up the notion of witness to include more than the original twelve disciples. Second, Paul introduces the deaths of some of the witnesses, a point to which he will return later in the chapter. Third, it prepares the way for Paul's account of his own experience of the risen Christ (v. 8).

In vv. 8-11 Paul reminds the Corinthians of his own history. According to external standards Paul has no qualifications to be an apostle and so he mentions himself at the end of the list. He was not one of the original Twelve, and indeed, was unfit to be an apostle because he persecuted the church. But as v. 10 makes clear, God and Jesus have surprising standards for apostolic vocation. By the grace of God Paul became an apostle, and by the grace of God Paul continues as an apostle. "Grace of God" has a double meaning in v. 10 for Paul. It is the gift of Paul's salvation and the gift that enables Paul to work.

Paul concludes in v. 11 by returning the focus to the Corinthians themselves. It does not matter whether Paul or someone else preached the gospel to the Corinthians. As vv. 3-5 show, all share the same core of good news. What matters is that it is this proclamation that has brought the Corinthians to faith.

The focus on Paul's call and vocation in vv. 8-10 provides suggestive links with the Old Testament and Gospel lessons. In all three lessons, the decision to live out one's faith comes in response to the initiating grace of God. Paul names that grace explicitly; the Isaiah and Luke texts illustrate that grace through their stories.

Sixth Sunday after the Epiphany

Lutheran	Roman Catholic	Episcopal	Revised Common
Jer. 17:5-8	Jer. 17:5-8	Jer. 17:5-10	Jer. 17:5-10
1 Cor. 15:12, 16-20	1 Cor. 15:12, 16-20	1 Cor. 15:12-20	1 Cor. 15:12-20
Luke 6:17-26	Luke 6:17, 20-26	Luke 6:17-26	Luke 6:17-26

The Gospel lesson is the first in a series of three Sunday lessons that read through the entirety of the Sermon on the Plain (Luke 6:20-49). This Sunday's lesson contains the blessings and woes with which the sermon begins. The Old Testament lesson from Jeremiah 17 is an example of the blessing and curse tradition that lies behind the blessings and woes of Luke 6. The epistle lesson continues the readings from 1 Corinthians 15.

GOSPEL: LUKE 6:17-26

Luke 6:17-19 serves as the introduction to the sermon that follows in vv. 20-49. It has the form of a summary of Jesus' ministry activity (cf. 4:14-15, 40-41). Verse 17a links the introduction to the preceding unit, Jesus' mountaintop retreat and his selection of the twelve apostles (6:12-16). It is important to remember that for Luke, "apostle" refers to the select group of twelve and "disciple" refers to the larger group of Jesus' followers. The sermon will be addressed to this larger group ("his disciples," v. 20). In addition to a great crowd of disciples, in v. 17 Luke also mentions a great multitude who have come to Jesus from all over the region. Not only do Jews from Judea and Jerusalem come to Jesus (who is presumably still in Galilee, cf. 7:1), but people from the Gentile regions of Tyre and Sidon in Phoenicia. The universal ministry Jesus promised in Luke 4:16-30 is already under way.

Verses 18-19 describe the motivation for the crowd's presence. They want to hear Jesus' word and experience Jesus' deeds (vv. 18b-19). This combination of word and deed fits with Luke's characterization of Jesus as "a prophet mighty in deed and word before God and all the people" (Luke 24:19; see also Luke 7:16; 13:33; Acts 3:22-26; 10:38). These introductory verses thus establish the sermon that follows as the words of a prophet.

The Sermon on the Plain (which derives its name from the reference to "a level place" in v. 17) is the Lukan version of the Sermon on the Mount

39

(Matthew 5–7). While there is tremendous overlap between the two sermons, the Lukan version is much shorter than Matthew's (30 verses to Matthew's 107). Each sermon contains traditional sayings and teachings of Jesus, but the composition of these sayings into a whole reflects the theological and/or pastoral needs and intent of each evangelist. Each Gospel presents the sermon as sample preaching of the Jesus depicted in its pages, and it is therefore important for the preacher to take each sermon on its own terms. It may be tempting to supplement the shorter Lukan version with teachings from the Sermon on the Mount, but to do so is to lose the voice of the Lukan Jesus.

The beginning of the two sermons is a case in point. Both sermons begin with a series of blessings, but the differences between the two outweigh their similarities. Matthew contains nine blessings, Luke four. The content of the four blessings they share (Matt. 5:3, 4, 6, 11-12; Luke 6:20-23) differs, because Matthew emphasizes the spiritual disposition, whereas Luke emphasizes material inequities (e.g., "the poor in spirit," Matt. 3:3; "the poor," Luke 6:20). Luke balances the blessings with a series of woes that are completely absent in Matthew, and these woes change the function of the blessings.

"Woe" is an expression of pain or displeasure. By beginning this sermon with blessings and woes, the Lukan Jesus positions himself in the blessing/curse tradition that goes back to the Law (e.g., Deuteronomy 27–28) and the Prophets (e.g., Jer. 17:5-8). Blessings and woes also figure prominently in the wisdom tradition. The form of the beginning of the sermon thus fits the speech of "a prophet mighty in deed and word."

The blessings (vv. 20-23) and woes (vv. 24-26) are a tightly constructed and balanced unit. There are four blessings and four woes, and each blessing is matched point for point in one of the woes. The corresponding blessings and woes are:

Blessing	Woe
v. 20	v. 24
v. 21a	v. 25a
v. 21b	v. 25b
vv. 22-23	v. 26

The transition from blessing to woe is marked by the adversative "but" in v. 24. (In Greek, the strong adversative *plān* is used.) The blessings and woes are cast in the second person plural. This means that Jesus' audience contained recipients of both blessing and woe. Jesus lays out a radical picture of faithfulness in vv. 20-23 that must have run counter to the assumptions of those addressed in vv. 24-26. Because the blessings and woes are so tightly paired, we will move through the text a pair at a time rather than verse by verse.

The first blessing/woe pair (vv. 20, 24) is built around the rich/poor antithesis. As noted earlier, the Lukan Jesus is concerned in v. 20 with physical poverty and material deprivation. Jesus does not point to a future reward for the poor but to a present one, "yours *is* the kingdom of God." The significance of the relationship between present and future is brought into even sharper relief by the partner woe in v. 24. The rich, by virtue of their wealth, have already used up their consolation. Thus wealth brings the rich nothing but woe, but the poor experience the kingdom of God. This contrast between rich and poor is a hallmark of Lukan theology. For Luke, wealth and possessions stand in the way of a person's full access to the kingdom of God

The second blessing/woe pair (vv. 21*a*, 25*a*) contrasts "you who hunger *now*" and "you who are full *now*." Again the emphasis is on the present life. How one lives in the present is the mark of one's relationship to God and to one another, not what awaits in some distant future. The antithesis of v. 21*a* and v. 25*a* is simple and direct; the status of those who are hungry and full will be reversed. The rich/poor and hungry/full antitheses recall Mary's words in the Magnificat, "He has filled the hungry with good things, and sent the rich empty away" (Luke 1:53).

The antithesis of the third blessing/woe pair (vv. 21*b*, 25*b*) is also simple and direct: you who weep *now* will laugh; and you who laugh *now* will mourn and weep. Again the emphasis falls on the present life and the impact of present behavior on one's future. Jesus' words are a stark reminder that one's assumptions about the future cannot be held distinct from the present conditions of a person's life (cf. the parable of the rich man and Lazarus, Luke 16:19-31). All three woes of vv. 24-25 suggest that if one squanders or hoards one's gifts in the present, they are gone, never to be retrieved or reclaimed (cf. the parable of the man with many barns, Luke 12:13-21).

The fourth blessing/woe pair (vv. 22-23; 26) is more complex and of slightly different character from the three preceding pairs. The first three pairs describe the disposition of true discipleship; this final pair focuses on the cost of discipleship. Verse 22 inventories some of the elements of religious persecution—hatred, exclusion, reviling, defaming—and attempts to uphold the embattled disciple by linking this rejection with the rejection of the prophets. Verse 22 probably has in view the Christians in Luke's own time who were persecuted because of their Christian identity ("for the sake of the Son of Man"). Verse 26 consolidates all the forms of persecution listed in v. 22 into the antithetical expression, "woe to you when all speak well of you." That is, woe to you when you risk nothing and stand for nothing that will offend anyone. The false prophets were careful to offend no one in power (cf. Isa. 30:10-11; Jer. 5:31; 6:13-14; 23:16-17).

These pairs of blessings and woes give the Sermon on the Plain a powerful beginning. Jesus' ministry and his vision of social reality shaped by the kingdom of God will entail radical social inversion and reversal. There is nothing spiritualized about these blessings and woes. Rather, they reflect on discipleship lived out in a concrete social reality. The promises and blessings are great, but so is the cost. The Sermon on the Plain continues the vision first celebrated by Mary when she contemplated Jesus' birth (Luke 1:46-55) and first articulated by Jesus in his sermon in the Nazareth synagogue (Luke 4:16-19; see the Third Sunday after the Epiphany).

FIRST LESSON: JEREMIAH 17:5-8

Jeremiah 17:5-8 is one in a series of collected sayings that comprise Jer. 17:5-13 (vv. 5-8; 9-10; 11; 12-13). These verses reflect the wisdom tradition that contrast two ways of life: life with God and life without God. These verses seem to be derived from Psalm 1 (see esp. v. 3), but the metaphors of Jer. 17:5-8 are much more vivid and fully developed than those in the Psalm.

As in the Lukan blessings and woes, the curse and blessing in the Jeremiah text are the mirror image of one another and have the same structure. Each verse opens with a general statement (vv. 5, 7) which is expanded with a horticultural metaphor (vv. 6, 8). The difference between being cursed or blessed is the character of a person's relationship with God. The cursed ones are those who place their trust in human beings and institutions and turn away from God. While the description of the cursed ones is a generalized wisdom saying, it also has particular relevance for Judah's political situation. The Judean kings who court competing alliances with Egypt and Babylon are trusting humans more than God.

The metaphor of v. 6 depicts the fate of those who do not place their trust in God. The metaphors revolve around the lack of water and nourishment. It is important to remember Judah's climate when reading this verse. Judah depended on rainfall and the reserves collected in cisterns for its water supply (cf. Jer. 2:13). Lack of water was often a real possibility. The people to whom these words were addressed thus knew all too vividly what it meant for a shrub to be without water in the desert, to be parched in the salty terrain.

The ones who are blessed, conversely, are those who trust in God. Whereas v. 5 gave three different descriptions of lack of trust ("trust in mere mortals," "make flesh their strength," "whose hearts turn away from

God"), v. 7 simply repeats the same basic truth twice. Trust in God is the single determinant of the course of one's life. The metaphors used to describe the life of the blessed are the exact opposite of those in v. 6. Whereas v. 6 used images of parched, desert places, v. 8 uses images of water and fruitfulness. The "tree" of the blessed will never be without water, because it is rooted in the right place. To trust in God is like being rooted near a stream, where water is available at all times, regardless of climatic changes.

The independent saying of vv. 9-10 is positioned as a commentary on vv. 5-8. Its acknowledgment of the perversity of the human heart (v. 9) leads to a statement about God's testing (v. 10). Positioned after vv. 5-8, these verses affirm that the alternative fates of the cursed and blessed are an outgrowth of the decisions the human heart has made about God.

In both the Lukan text and this Jeremiah text, a connection is made between deeds and consequences. That is, the choices one makes about relationship to God and to humans do and will effect the future direction of one's life. To set one's trust in "mere flesh" (e.g., in the wealth or abundance of food in Luke 6:24-25), is to shut oneself from the kingdom of God. Neither the curse of Jer. 17:5-6 nor the woes of Luke 6:24-26 are punitive. Rather, they give a vivid theological rendering of the consequences when human beings remove their trust from God and hence move themselves away from God's blessings.

SECOND LESSON: 1 CORINTHIANS 15:12-20

In 1 Cor. 15:1-11 (see the Fifth Sunday after the Epiphany) Paul reminded the Corinthians of the good news that stands at the core of their faith: the death and resurrection of Christ. The recital of the creed thus served as a reminder of what all Christians affirm and hold in common. Paul's opening statement in 15:12a ("if Christ is proclaimed as raised from the dead") recalls the truth of the central creed. Yet even in the face of the core proclamation of Christ's resurrection from the dead, some of the Corinthians say "there is no resurrection of the dead" (v. 12b). In vv. 13-19 Paul shows that this claim can be maintained only at the expense of the core gospel.

How one understands this Corinthian contention about the resurrection depends on where one places the emphasis: no *resurrection* of the dead or no resurrection of the *dead*. The remainder of chap. 15 suggests that the emphasis should be on "dead," that is, on death as the prerequisite for the resurrection. Read in this way, the Corinthians' claim of v. 12b is a belief in the present actualization of the resurrection, a belief that the Corinthians already fully experience Christ's resurrection without having experienced death. The Corinthians' dismissal of death as a prerequisite for resurrection explains Paul's use of the creed in 15:3ff. Paul's presentation of the common gospel focuses on death (vv. 3 and 4*a*) as much as on resurrection (vv. 4*b* and 5) and clearly positions Christ's death as a prerequisite to his resurrection.

In vv. 13-14 Paul draws out the implications of the Corinthians' denial of the resurrection of the dead. If they deny the resurrection of the dead, they deny Christ's resurrection (v. 13). The Corinthian contention thus invalidates the death and resurrection of Christ. And if they invalidate the death and resurrection of Christ, then Paul's proclamation and the Corinthians' faith are both "in vain" (v. 14). Paul framed his earlier recital of the gospel with references to the Corinthians' faith (15:2, 11). To deny the relationship between death and resurrection puts that faith in jeopardy.

Verse 15 draws out a further implication of the Corinthians' denial: If what some Corinthians claim is true, then Paul must be "misrepresenting God," because again, as 15:3ff. show, the core gospel testifies to God's involvement in the resurrection of Christ. God's involvement is shown in two ways: (1) by the passive verb "was raised" in v. 4*b*; and (2) in the references to Scripture in vv. 3 and 4. The references to Scripture show that the death and resurrection of Christ was part of God's plan of salvation. When the Corinthians deny the resurrection of the dead, therefore, they are calling God's plan into question.

Verse 16 makes clear that the focus of the Corinthians' denial is on death as a prerequisite for resurrection: "For if the *dead* are not raised, then Christ has not been raised." In v. 17 Paul moves the focus away from the gospel and onto the Corinthians' faith. To deny death as a prerequisite for resurrection implies denying Christ's death as a prerequisite for his resurrection, and since Christ "died for our sins" (15:3), the Corinthians are in essence denying the very source of their redemption.

Verse 18 alludes to a second controversy in the Corinthian church: whether those who have already died will be able to participate in the coming kingdom (see esp. 15:20-28). This controversy is related to the central denial of death as a prerequisite for resurrection. If the resurrection is already fully actualized in the present, then there is no need for a future resurrection, and those who are already dead "have perished" with no share in God's coming kingdom.

The key to Paul's understanding of the resurrection is in v. 19, with its emphasis on "for this life only." This verse makes two critical theological affirmations. First, Paul affirms the reality of the future dimension of Christian existence. If we restrict Christ to the present, "we are of all people most to be pitied." The Christian gospel is not restricted to the present (as some Corinthians assert with their claim to experience already the fullness of the resurrection). Notice, however, that Paul does not put all the emphasis on the future, either, as many contemporary Christian affirmations of heaven and the resurrection do. Paul holds the present and future together in the resurrection promise. One does indeed hope in Christ for this life, but not for this life only.

Second, v. 19 affirms the importance of hope in the Christian life and makes clear the grounds of Christian hope. Hope is not simply a reworking of present thought and experience (see also Rom. 8:24-25), but a genuine hope that is open to the possibility of the future. "If for this life only we have hoped in Christ," we limit both the present and the future, because there can be no *present* hope without faith in the possibility of a *future*. To limit hope in Christ to the present is to limit the possibilities of God to what we see before us day after day; to be open to a future in Christ means that each present moment carries in it the seeds of transformation and new life. To limit hope in Christ to the future, conversely, also denies the present, because it positions the present only as something to be endured until the future arrives. Paul's expression "for this life only" holds the present and future in a delicate balance that reflects the reality of Christian hope: the present and future bound in an indissoluble relationship by the power of the resurrection. The Christian present moves toward the possibilities of the future, and the Christian future transforms the impossibilities of the present.

Seventh Sunday after the Epiphany

Lutheran	Roman Catholic	Episcopal	Revised Common
Gen. 45:3-8a, 15	1 Sam. 26:2, 7-9, 12-13, 22-23	Gen. 45:3-11, 21-28	Gen. 45:3-11, 15
1 Cor. 15:35-38a, 42-50	1 Cor. 15:45-49	1 Cor. 15:35-38, 42-50	1 Cor. 15:35-38, 42-50
Luke 6:27-38	Luke 6:27-38	Luke 6:27-38	Luke 6:27-38

The Gospel lesson continues the reading of Jesus' Sermon on the Plain. The focus of this portion of the sermon (6:27-38) is on what it means to love one's enemies, and the Old Testament lesson (Genesis 45 or 1 Samuel 26) illustrates that theme. The Old Testament lessons are powerful stories in which the central character does indeed love his enemy, and that love has transformative power. The epistle lesson continues Paul's discussion of the resurrection in 1 Corinthians 15.

GOSPEL: LUKE 6:27-38

The material in Luke 6:27-38 overlaps with material found in Matthew 5–7, but Luke groups the pieces of Jesus tradition in an order different from Matthew. This different ordering results in different emphases in Matthew and Luke. Two differences are especially significant for the interpretation of Luke 6:27-38. First, the "love your enemies" teaching in Matt. 5:43-44 occurs in the middle of a section (5:39-48), but in Luke 6:27-28 is positioned as the beginning of the section. In Luke this teaching thus serves to announce the theme of the section. Second, the "Golden Rule" occurs in a section unrelated to the love of enemies in Matthew (7:12) and is offered as a summary of the Law and the Prophets. In Luke, that teaching is specifically located as commentary on the command to love one's enemies (6:31). As shall be seen below, this move makes the command of the "Golden Rule" even more radical.

"Love your enemies" is the central command in vv. 27-28 around which the other three commands cluster. These commands ("do good . . . ," "bless . . . ," "pray for . . .") focus the words about loving your enemy on the specific enemies with which the Christian community was faced. The references to those who hate, curse, and abuse recall the blessing of Luke 6:22. This focus of the supplemental commands in vv. 27-28 does not restrict the scope of Jesus' words by naming one type of enemy. Rather, this specificity renders the call of Jesus' command even more challenging. "Love your enemies" is not a theoretical imperative but is an imperative addressed to the realities of the community's life.

Jesus' commands in v. 29 also focus on specific situations in which one is called to love one's enemies. The first command, to offer the other cheek, is a call for civil and social disobedience in the presence of one's enemy. To slap someone in the face was a way for a social superior to discipline or punish a social inferior. To turn the other cheek in that context is to deny power to the social superior. The second command probably refers to a court setting. This is clearer in Matt. 5:40, which reads, "If anyone wants to sue you and take your coat, give your cloak as well." When a debtor was sued in court, he gave his coat as a pledge for his debts (Exod. 22:25-27; Deut. 24:10-13, 7; Amos 2:7-8). What Jesus commands here is to go beyond the requirements of the law and give your shirt as well as your coat, not as an act of self-denial but of civil disobedience. If one gives one's shirt, one would stand naked in court, drawing attention to the harshness of calling in the debts. (For a full discussion of the civil implications of these verses, see Walter Wink, *Engaging the Powers: Discernment and Resistance in World Domination* [Minneapolis: Fortress Press, 1992], 175–86.) By dropping the explicit reference to legal proceedings in this verse, Luke again makes the command more radical. Civil disobedience to the abuse of power is not restricted to a specific legal setting, but holds for more general social settings of power inequities as well. Both commands in v. 29 serve to undercut the apparent power of one's enemy, and are thus very subversive enactments of the "love one's enemy" command.

The Lukan version of the Jesus saying in v. 30 also renders it more socially radical than the Matthean form (cf. Matt. 5:42). The translation of this verse is a bit misleading, because the verb translated "beg" simply means "ask," and may imply all situations of asking, not simply almsgiving. Verse 30*b* supports a broader reading of the verb. If one's giving were simply almsgiving, one would not expect to get one's things back. Verse 30 must therefore refer to broader situations of borrowing and debt. What Jesus suggests here is that members of the Christian community are not to follow the social and economic *status quo*, creating power imbalances through the disposition of goods like those alluded to in v. 29. Instead the community is to see goods as something to be shared, not as a means of power and social control. It is the vision of the Jubilee (cf. 6:35 and Wink, *Engaging the Powers*).

This context suggests that Luke understands the "Golden Rule" (v. 31) to be about more than reciprocal relationships. It is framed by verses that exhort a much more radical behavior (vv. 27-30; 32-35). In the context of loving one's enemies, to "do to others as you would have them do to you" means to exercise reciprocity with one's enemies; to love one's enemies involves not becoming an enemy oneself (v. 30).

Jesus puts the Golden Rule to the test in vv. 32-35. In three parallel conditional statements ("if you," vv. 32, 33, 34), Jesus measures the Golden Rule against his initial imperative, "Love your enemies." In each of the three conditions, to exercise reciprocity with one's colleagues is not enough. Even sinners—that is, those in a broken relationship with God—do that much. Jesus calls "you that listen" to a much broader and hence more radical social program: "But love your enemies, do good, and lend, expecting nothing in return" (v. 35c). The reward (v. 35b) for such behavior will not be calculated according to the currency of the economic and social systems of the day (cf. "what credit is that to you," vv. 33, 34) but will be calculated in terms of the community's relationship to God. Their reward will be a new identity, "children of the Most High."

In v. 36 Jesus provides the ultimate theological grounding for the community behavior to which he calls his audience. Their actions ("be merciful") are grounded in the very character of God ("just as your Father is merciful"). The mercy of God is well documented in the Old Testament (Exod. 34:6; Deut. 4:31; Joel 2:13; Jonah 4:2). Thus the bottom line command is not, "Do to others as you would have them do to you," but "Do to others as God has done and is doing to you and to them."

In addition to concluding vv. 27-35, v. 36 also introduces vv. 37-38. The four imperatives in these two verses (two negative and two positive) are imperatives that, if enacted, will show that the community does indeed live out the mercy of God. Each of the four imperatives is paired with its consequences for the community. The pairs make clear that as the community acts, so shall they receive. This is brought out explicitly in v. 38. Verse 38 also makes clear that Jesus does not envision stingy, closed acts of giving and forgiving from the community. Rather, Jesus envisions generosity whose abundance pushes at the very capacities of language. The language used to describe the "good measure" in v. 38 is as exuberant as the gifts of which it speaks: "pressed down, shaken together, running over." When the community gives, it will receive gifts almost beyond measure. In 6:27-38 Jesus commands a pattern of community life, grounded in the love of one's enemies and the mercy of God, which will flood the community with abundance.

FIRST LESSON: GENESIS 45:3-11, 15

Genesis 45 narrates Joseph's disclosure of his identity to his brothers (45:4-12). It is a moment fraught with tension, because ever since Joseph's brothers journeyed to Egypt in search of food (Genesis 42), the reader has wondered how the final scene will be played out. From the beginning Joseph had the advantage with his brothers, because he recognized them but they did not recognize him (42:8). Joseph repeatedly tested his brothers: imprisoning them as spies (42:14-17), placing money in their sacks (42:25, 43:20-25), planting a silver cup among Benjamin's possessions (44:1-6). The brothers find themselves completely at Joseph's mercy when chapter 45 opens: He has the power to enslave or release Benjamin and hence the power to repay his brothers in kind for their treatment of him. His brothers had clearly acted towards him as enemy, selling him into slavery (37:25-28). The choice before Joseph, therefore, is how he will act toward his enemies: with love or with vengeance.

The pain of the moment is too much for Joseph (45:1) and he cannot keep his identity secret any longer. But even when his identity is revealed to his brothers, the question still remains: How will Joseph act toward his enemies? His brothers know this is the question because "they could not answer him, so dismayed were they at his presence" (45:3).

The answer to the question comes in vv. 4-15: Joseph will love his enemies. When he speaks to his brothers, his words are full of grace and forgiveness. He expresses no rancor, no vindictiveness, no hatred. Instead he depicts for his brothers how the providence of God worked through their act "to preserve life" (45:5). The brothers thought that they had sold their brother, but in reality God, through the brothers, had found a way to keep the people of Israel alive (45:7-8). Joseph's speech expresses one of the central themes of the Joseph narrative, the sometime hiddenness of God's acts within human history. When paired with the Gospel lesson for this Sunday, however, his speech also bears eloquent witness to the transformative power of loving one's enemies.

Everything about Joseph's relationship with his brothers is made new because of his act of love. Joseph is reconciled with his brothers. A new future is offered to the brothers, one marked by prosperity and abundance (45:16-24), and Jacob is given a peace he had long stopped thinking possible (45:28; cf. 37:35). All this, because Joseph was able to love his enemies. He did not hold tightly to his position and power and use it to dominate his brothers, but chose instead to act toward them in love as God had acted toward him.

ROMAN CATHOLIC FIRST LESSON: 1 SAMUEL 26:1-25

1 Samuel 26:1-25 also narrates a powerful story of loving one's enemies. In this story, David, who Saul has been trying to kill, comes upon Saul sleeping in his encampment (1 Sam. 26:7; cf. 23:15—24:22). In a speech

that sets the issue for the entire story, Abishai says to David, "God has given your enemy into your hand today" (26:8) and asks David's permission to kill Saul. David refuses to allow Saul, indisputably his mortal enemy, to be killed because Saul is God's anointed king and to act against Saul would be to act against God. It is a powerful moment in which David allows the character of God to determine his response to his enemy. David takes Saul's spear and water jar as a sign of Saul's vulnerability and David's graciousness (26:12-13).

When David speaks to Saul later (26:21-25), David makes explicit that his actions were guided by the character of God. He held Saul's life to be precious as God holds life to be precious. Like the Genesis 45 story, 1 Samuel 26 is a vivid illustration of Jesus' words in Luke 6. David does not act out of hate toward his enemy, the one who hates him (see 1 Sam. 18:29; 19:10). Instead he does good to the one who hates him. He is merciful because God is merciful.

SECOND LESSON: 1 CORINTHIANS 15:35-38, 42-50

Paul begins a new section in his discussion of the resurrection at 1 Corinthians 15:35. He introduces this new section with two rhetorical questions that the rest of the section tries to answer. The epithet "Fool!" (v. 36) seems to indicate that some of the Corinthians felt that the questions Paul asks in v. 35 were the very questions that would baffle Paul and so prove that he was wrong about the resurrection and they were right. Instead of being baffled by their questions, however, Paul is able to provide several answers to them.

His first response (vv. 36-38) answers the questions with the agricultural imagery of sowing (cf. John 12:24). Paul uses this imagery to show that in nature, a seed must change in order to produce a plant. It must be buried in the ground (die) before it can be born into a new state. Each seed will have a body given by God according to its own type as it grows into its new life. Paul thus emphasizes: (1) the necessity of death as a prerequisite for resurrection; and (2) the discontinuity between the present and future life. Both these points build on his argument in 15:12-20: future life is not fully actualized in the present.

In Paul's second answer (vv. 39-44), he addresses the question of "what kind of body." This is a complex answer in which Paul moves from flesh to body to glory. The reference to different kinds of flesh in v. 39 recalls the creation story. The next step in his argument compares different kinds of bodies, heavenly and earthly, each with its own kind of glory. This, too, recalls Genesis 1. There are different glories (v. 41), just as there are different kinds of flesh. Paul thus argues from creation to show that different kinds of flesh and bodies are possible and indeed necessary. Verse 42*a* makes this point explicit: as there are different natural bodies, so it is with the resurrection of the dead.

A rhetorically polished section of antitheses (vv. 42*b*-44) provides Paul's third answer. These antitheses build on Paul's earlier use of sowing imagery, for each of them portrays the changes from what is sown to what is raised:

Sown: perishable	*Raised:* imperishable
dishonor	glory
weakness	power
physical body	spiritual body

Each of these antitheses is theologically more complex, culminating in the physical body/spiritual body contrast.

Verse 45 begins Paul's fourth answer (vv. 45-49) in which Paul uses the creation of Adam (Gen. 2:7) to build his argument about the resurrection body. The first Adam was "a living being," the second Adam (Christ) a "life-giving spirit." This Adam/Christ typology, so important in other parts of Paul (Rom. 5:12-21), works here to show that there are two kinds of creation, physical and spiritual. Verses 46-49 address the relationship between these two creations: The physical must precede the spiritual and that order cannot be reversed. Adam was first from the earth, Christ was second from heaven (v. 47), and the descendants of Adam and Christ must maintain the same order and relationship to one another (vv. 48-49): earthly first, then heavenly. Adam and Christ are both prototypes for Christian existence: "We have borne the image of the man of dust; we will also bear the image of the man of heaven."

The order of the verbs in v. 49 and their tenses are important: borne, will bear. The full share in Christ's resurrection is still in the future. The answer to Paul's questions in v. 35 thus derives ultimately from Christ's death and resurrection. If resurrection was possible for Christ, it will be possible for the Christian community. But this resurrection must always be understood in the context of Christ's experience as proclaimed in the creed (15:3-5): death first, then resurrection. The answer to the questions of "how" in v. 35 is through the example of God in Christ.

Eighth Sunday after the Epiphany

Lutheran	Roman Catholic	Episcopal	Revised Common
Jer. 7:1-7 (8-15)	Sir. 27:4-7	Jer. 7:1-7 (8-15)	Sir. 27:4-7 or Isa. 55:10-13
1 Cor. 15:51-58	1 Cor. 15:54-58	1 Cor. 15:50-58	1 Cor. 15:51-58
Luke 6:39-49	Luke 6:39-45	Luke 6:39-49	Luke 6:39-49

The Gospel lesson concludes the Sermon on the Plain. The focus of the concluding section is on the relationship between a person's words and deeds. The four lectionaries offer a variety of readings for the first lesson; each of them complements the Gospel lesson by continuing the word/ deeds theme. The epistle lesson is Paul's eloquent conclusion to his discussion of the resurrection in 1 Corinthians 15.

GOSPEL: LUKE 6:39-49

Before focusing on the conclusion of the Sermon on the Plain, it is useful to review its overall contents and movement. The sermon opened with an introductory litany of blessings and woes (6:20-26; the Sixth Sunday after the Epiphany) that grounds the sermon in Jesus' theological vision of community and social transformation. In 6:27-38 (the Seventh Sunday after the Epiphany), with its focus on loving one's enemies, Jesus articulated a community ethic that makes his vision of social transformation possible. In the conclusion of the sermon (6:39-49) Jesus addresses the relationship between his teaching and the disciples' actions. Luke 6:39-49 shares many Jesus traditions with Matthew 7, (6:41-42 = Matt. 7:3-5; 6:43-44 = Matt. 7:16-20; 6:64 = Matt. 7:21; 6:47-49 = Matt. 7:47-49), but the Lukan grouping differs from the order in Matthew. In addition, Luke includes Jesus sayings in the sermon that appear elsewhere in Matthew (6:39 = Matt. 5:14; 6:40 = Matt. 10:24-25). When Luke 6:39-49 is compared with Matthew 7, the distinctive Lukan emphasis emerges. Whereas the Sermon on the Mount concludes by stressing the need for hearers of the word to become doers of the word, Luke presents a slightly more complex relationship between hearing and doing. Disciples of Jesus' word are those who are themselves willing to be taught (6:39-40) and whose actions derive from what they have been taught (6:41-49). The conclusion of the Sermon on the Plain stresses that doing the word does not mean the end of hearing the word.

The parable and its interpretation (6:39-40) with which this section of the sermon begins makes the balance between hearing and doing clear. The parable is vivid in its succinctness: Jesus holds up the image of one blind leader and one blind follower heading toward a pit. As is often the case with Jesus' parables, Jesus does not answer the question the parable poses (e.g., Luke 15:3-10), because the way the parable is framed makes the answer apparent. A blind leader is no good to a blind follower; both will end up in the pit. The interpretation of the parable in v. 40 suggests that the blind leader is to be understood as a disciple who stands in the place of the teacher. The word *disciple* comes from the root "to learn" in Greek, so that the most basic definition of a disciple is one who learns. A disciple cannot possibly lead until he or she has been taught; to attempt to lead without having been taught is to confuse the role of disciple and teacher. As the parable of v. 39 suggests, this confusion places the life of the community in jeopardy. The expression "fully qualified" does not refer to a person's inherent qualifications, as the ambiguous English wording might suggest. A clearer translation would read, "Everyone who is fully trained will be like the teacher."

The figurative language in vv. 41-42 provides another illustration of the cost when someone attempts to teach without first giving heed to the teaching of oneself. The images of specks and logs in the eye continue the theme of blindness from v. 39. This saying about the log and speck is used to counter judgmentalism in the community in Matt. 7:3-5, but Luke uses this saying to further his point about teaching. Before one can teach others how to live ("Friend, let me take out the speck in your eye"), one must first reshape one's own life ("first take the log out of your own eye"). To teach others about specks while one's own vision is impaired by a log is again the blind teaching the blind.

The image of fruit in vv. 43-44 develops the relationship between who a person is and what a person does. The image is based on a horticultural reality: The fruit a tree bears is the decisive mark of the type and quality of the tree. A tree before it bears fruit may be hard to distinguish from another tree: Is it a healthy tree or a diseased tree? Is it an apple or a pear tree? Is it a raspberry or blackberry bush? But when a tree bears fruit, all questions are answered. Healthy-looking foliage cannot disguise the bad fruit a tree bears; a tree that bears good fruit is a good tree regardless of the appearance of its limbs and foliage.

In v. 45 Jesus explicitly interprets the tree/fruit metaphors as they pertain to human identity and actions. What a person says is always a reflection of who a person is. "The good treasure of the heart," "the abundance of the heart" are the human equivalents of a good tree. What a person says and does is the good fruit of this good tree. When vv. 43-45 are read in conjunction with vv. 39-42, Jesus is heard urging his disciples to teach out of the goodness of their hearts; to demonstrate that they are indeed a good tree by teaching in order to produce good, not to condemn, belittle, or misguide.

Verses 46-49 give an urgency to Jesus' words. It is not enough to acknowledge one's loyalty to Jesus ("Lord, Lord") without enacting Jesus' words (v. 46). If one comes to Jesus and hears, and translates that hearing into actions, it is as if one built a house that will withstand the destructive power of a flood (v. 48). If one hears Jesus but does not act, the words provide no support against the flood's destructive power (v. 49). One has only to revisit the destruction of the 1993 Mississippi River flood to visualize the contrast Jesus lays out here. The contrast of these verses is often misread or misapplied in popular interpretation, however. This well-known parable is often interpreted as saying that life in Jesus' word is life lived on a rock-solid foundation; life without Jesus' word is life lived on a shaky foundation. But this is not the contrast of these verses. It is not Jesus' words alone that provide the solid foundation; it is the disciples' enacted response to those words. The ones who hear and act build a solid foundation for themselves because they enact Jesus' vision of a new social and community reality. They do live in a house built on a deep, rock-solid foundation, because they live on the foundation of love of one's enemies (vv. 27-36), abundant giving (v. 38), and informed teaching (vv. 39-42).

The Sermon on the Plain thus ends with Jesus directing his disciples, "those who listen" (v. 27), to take a good look at themselves and their relationships to those within their own community. Are they enacting what they have heard? Are they reshaping their own lives in accordance with Jesus' words before they demand reform of others? This concluding emphasis of Jesus' sermon is an important word for the Christian community. Hearing and doing reside in a delicate balance; to hear without doing or to do without continuing to hear and be taught puts the church at risk. The "foundation" of the church is threatened when disciples teach without continuing to allow themselves to be taught, when disciples think of themselves solely as teachers instead of as disciples engaged in training (v. 40).

FIRST LESSON: JEREMIAH 7:1-7

The theme of the interrelationship of word and deed continues in Jer. 7:1-7. This passage is the beginning of Jeremiah's temple sermon, in which Jeremiah proclaims that faithful words without faithful actions are meaningless before God. Jeremiah preaches his sermon as a result of God's command (vv. 1-2). The physical setting of this sermon is an essential part of its meaning: Jeremiah is commissioned by God "to stand in the gate of the Lord's house" and call Judah to repentance. The temple was understood as the symbol of God's abiding presence, God's unconditional support of the people of Judah. By preaching this sermon at the gates of the temple, Jeremiah calls that basic theological presupposition into question.

The challenge of Jeremiah's sermon is proclaimed in vv. 3-4. Verse 3 states the challenge positively: Judah needs to amend its ways, change its action. If they do that, God's presence with them in their land will continue. Verse 3*b* is ambiguous in the Hebrew and can be translated two ways, "and let me dwell with you in this place" (NRSV) or "and I will let you dwell in this place" (NRSV variant, RSV; cf. NIV). The translation difference is a matter of focus and emphasis. The first translation ("let me dwell . . .") suggests that Judah's actions in and of themselves make it impossible for God to dwell with them in their land. This translation focuses directly on Judah's actions as the determining factor in God's presence with them. The second translation gives more explicit agency to God. Both translations point to the same result—unless the people of Judah change their ways, they will lose their land (cf. vv. 6-7). The first translation may more succinctly capture the mood of Jeremiah's words, because it points most directly to Judah's own decisions and actions as the cause of exile.

Verse 4 states the challenge of the sermon negatively: Judah is falsely reliant on the temple. Verse 4 is unremittingly negative about the power of the temple system and its liturgy. ("do not trust," "deceptive words"). The threefold repetition of "this is the temple of the Lord" mimics and mocks the words of the temple liturgy. The people of Judah can no longer hide behind the reassuring words of the temple service because these words have lulled them into complacency and unfaithfulness to the commands of God.

Verses 5-7 expand on the theme of v. 3, making more specific what Judah is called to do. These verses set up an "if-then" condition for staying in the land. The "if" (vv. 5-6), the amending of ways to which Judah is summoned, involves the renunciation of acts of social injustice and idolatry and the embrace of acts of justice. Verse 6 spells out the basic requirements of Torah obedience. The "then" is in v. 7. If Judah enacts the social and theological demands of Torah, then God will keep them in their land.

Judah has forgotten that the land is a gift (v. 7), and has acted instead as if the land were its guaranteed possession. But life in the land is a sign of the people's relationship with God, a relationship that they have neglected. They have assumed that the right words were all that was needed to maintain that relationship (v. 4; cf. Luke 6:46). In this sermon, Jeremiah reminds Judah that right actions are required.

ALTERNATIVE FIRST LESSON: SIRACH 27:4-7; ISAIAH 55:10-13

The lesson from Sirach is a wisdom text that uses a variety of images to show the necessity of testing the trustworthiness of a person's words. The lesson employs three metaphors—sieve (v. 4), kiln (v. 5), and fruit (v. 6)—that illustrate the aphorism stated directly in v. 7. The fruit metaphor belongs to the wisdom strain on which Jesus draws in Luke 6:43-45 and makes the same point: Words reveal a person's character.

The lesson from Isa. 55:10-13 also reflects on the relationship between word and deed, but in this case, the focus is on God's words and deeds. The vision of these verses is one of renewal and regeneration among God's people as a result of God's word (vv. 10-11). It provides an eschatological context for the Lukan lesson, locating Jesus' vision of the community's transformed life alongside God's vision of the new creation for God's people (vv. 12-13).

SECOND LESSON: 1 CORINTHIANS 15:51-58

The epistle lesson is the conclusion of Paul's discussion of the resurrection. These verses ground all that has preceded in the eschatological transformation that awaits God's people. The language in vv. 51-53 reflects the sense of apocalyptic immediacy that is at the heart of Paul's world view (cf. 15:20-28): God's new age will come quickly and will involve everyone, both the living and the dead. Those who have already died "will be raised imperishable" and those still alive "will be changed." The final answer to questions about the resurrection is that God is more powerful than death.

The act of transformation from a body still under the power of death (that is, mortal and imperishable), to a life wholly under the power of God (that is, imperishability and immortality), is the ultimate fulfillment of Scripture (vv. 54-55). In 15:3-4 Paul depicted Christ's death and resurrection as part of the fulfillment of Scripture, of God's plan for God's people, and now he depicts the general resurrection in the same terms. When mortality and perishability are denied their power by God, then death has lost all its power (Isa. 25:7; Hos. 13:14). In vv. 56-57 Paul points the Corinthians to the lingering power of death in their daily lives (sin, law) and hence to the areas where the victory that God has worked through Christ is at work in this life.

The exhortations of v. 58 are thus grounded in the assured victory of God in Christ. Paul moves his teaching on the resurrection, hope, and

God's future into the Corinthians' present lives. The exhortations of v. 58 are not random exhortations, but exhortations derived from the truth of the resurrection ("therefore"). The resurrection of God's victory over the power of death should equip the Corinthians to "be steadfast, immovable, always excelling in the work of the Lord." The work of the Lord is love and the edification of the community (1 Corinthians 12–14). As the debates of earlier sections of 1 Corinthians suggest (including earlier section of 1 Corinthians 15), the Corinthians sometimes stray from the work of love and edification. Paul therefore ends the exhortations with an appeal to what the Corinthians know, "that in the Lord your labor is not in vain."

The key word in this appeal is "in vain." First, this recalls 1 Corinthians 15:10, where Paul declared that God's grace toward him "has not been in vain." Paul's life in God is therefore an example to the Corinthians that they, too, can labor faithfully. Second, and more important, in 15:14 Paul told the Corinthians that if there were no resurrection of Christ, both his proclamation and their faith "has been in vain." But *because the resurrection of Christ is true*, they are not in vain. It is this knowledge, the knowledge of the death and resurrection of Christ with which Paul began 1 Corinthians 15, to which Paul makes appeal in v. 58. Because of the resurrection, the Corinthians can do that which Paul exhorts. Their labor is not in vain, because God's victory is assured.

1 Corinthians 15 thus ends with a powerful statement of hope, not an empty hope based on idle speculation about the future, but a hope that empowers and guides the Christian community in the present. We can do God's work in the present because the death and resurrection of Christ remind us that God's final victory over death is assured. Because we know that the future belongs to God, we are empowered to live the present in confidence, to show by our lives and labor that we trust what God has done in Jesus and is doing in us. As Paul wrote, "Thanks be to God, who gives us the victory through our Lord Jesus Christ" (v. 57).

The Transfiguration of Our Lord
Last Sunday after the Epiphany

Lutheran	Roman Catholic	Episcopal	Revised Common
Deut. 34:1-12	Dan. 7:9-10, 13-14	Exod. 34:29-35	Exod. 34:29-35
2 Cor. 4:3-6	2 Pet. 1:16-19	1 Cor. 12:27—13:13	1 Cor. 13:12—4:2
Luke 9:28-36	Luke 9:28b-36	Luke 9:28-36	Luke 9:28-36 (37-43)

Transfiguration Sunday marks the transition from the Sundays after the Epiphany to the season of Lent. The Gospel lesson returns to one of the central themes of the Epiphany, the manifestation of the light and glory of God in Jesus, but it situates that glory in the context of Jesus' upcoming passion and death (Luke 9:31). The Old Testament and epistle lessons vary widely across the four lectionaries, as each lectionary emphasizes a different aspect of the Transfiguration narrative.

GOSPEL: LUKE 9:28-36

The opening words of the Transfiguration narrative ("now about eight days after these sayings," v. 28), suggest that Luke does not intend the Transfiguration account to be read in isolation as a singular event in Jesus' ministry. Rather, the Transfiguration is to be read as a continuation of what preceded, and in particular, as commentary on the preceding sayings of Jesus.

The sayings to which Luke points the reader are Luke 9:18-22 and 9:23-27. Luke 9:18-22 contains Peter's confession of Jesus as the Messiah (v. 20). Jesus responds to Peter's confession with a command to keep silent (v. 21) and with the first of three passion predictions (v. 22; see also 9:43b-45; 18:31-34). This passion prediction is intended as a corrective to Peter's Messianic confession. Unless Peter understands the full course of Jesus' life and ministry, including his suffering, death, and resurrection, the title "Messiah" is empty. The passion prediction is followed by Jesus' teaching on the nature of discipleship (vv. 23-27). This teaching emphasizes the radical call and cost of following Jesus (vv. 23-25). Verses 26-27 give discipleship an eschatological dimension, because they link one's response to Jesus with the coming of the Son of Man in "glory" and the kingdom of God. By explicitly referring back to "these sayings" in 9:28, Luke sets up the Transfiguration to be interpreted in light of Jesus' passion, death, and resurrection and the nature of discipleship.

Luke 9:28 introduces several elements that set the stage for the event that follows. First, Jesus goes up to a mountain. The specific mountain is unimportant (and hence goes unmentioned by Luke). What is significant is the symbolism of a journey to a mountaintop as a move out of the ordinary to a place of revelation (cf. the Sinai tradition in Exodus). Second, for Luke in particular, a mountaintop is a place of prayer for Jesus (cf. 6:12; 22:39-40). In v. 28, Jesus withdraws to the mountain for communion with God. Third, Jesus takes his inner circle of disciples with him (cf. 8:51). The disciples, especially Peter, will play an important role as witnesses to the Transfiguration.

Verses 29-32 narrate the Transfiguration event proper. Significantly, the Transfiguration occurs while Jesus is at prayer (v. 29; cf. 3:21-22). Verse 29 depicts the visible signs of the Transfiguration in Jesus' own person. First, the "appearance of his face changed." The face is what distinguishes one person from another. For Jesus' face to change means that the markers to recognize Jesus have changed. This reference to Jesus' face may be an allusion to Exod. 34:29-35, in which Moses' face shines because he has been in the presence of God. Second, Jesus' clothes become "dazzling white." This combination of adjectives is used to depict the brilliance of Jesus' presence. Dazzling brilliance is an apocalyptic symbol for the presence of God (Ezek. 1:27-28; Dan. 10:6; Rev. 1:13-14; see also Mark 9:3).

In v. 30 Moses and Elijah appear with Jesus. The words "they saw" explicitly positions Peter, James, and John as witnesses to this appearance. Judaism around the time of Jesus invested the return of Moses and Elijah with messianic significance. Because Elijah was transported into heaven without dying (2 Kings 2:11), many Jews linked his return with the beginning of the messianic age. God's promises in Deut. 18:15 to raise up another prophet like Moses led to eschatological expectations of the return of Moses himself. The linking of Moses and Elijah with the transfigured Jesus on the mountaintop points to Jesus as the Messiah (cf. 9:18-22). Moses and Elijah may also represent the Law and the Prophets (cf. Luke 24:27).

That Moses and Elijah "appeared in glory" (v. 31) means that they (like Jesus in his brilliance) manifested the visible radiance and presence of God. Matthew (17:3) and Mark (9:4) simply recount that Moses and Elijah talk with Jesus, but Luke includes the substance of their conversation. Their conversation about Jesus' "departure" provides the decisive clue to interpreting the Lukan Transfiguration. The Greek word for departure is *exodos*, "exodus." This word works on the level of pure story line and geography; Jesus will soon "depart" for Jerusalem (cf. 9:51), but the Greek word also carries with it important associations from Israel's history. This reference to exodus recalls Israel's Exodus from Egypt to the promised land, and positions Jesus' "exodus" as another exodus for liberation.

With this symbolic reading of exodus in view, the reference to Jerusalem in 9:31*b* becomes even more significant. Not only does the reference to Jerusalem anticipate Jesus' journey to Jerusalem that will begin at 9:51, but it builds on the passion prediction in 9:21-22 to point to Jesus' death in Jerusalem (cf. 13:34). Jesus' passion and death belong to the exodus of liberation. In addition, since 9:21-22 also predicted Jesus' resurrection, the reference to Jesus' departure in 9:31 also probably implies his resurrection and ascension (Luke 24:51). The Transfiguration story is thus linked by Luke to Jesus' death, resurrection, and ascension. That Moses and Elijah talk with Jesus about his departure suggests that Jesus' passion, death, and resurrection are grounded in the law and the prophets as part of God's plan for God's people.

Verses 32-33 focus on the disciples' and Peter's response to the mountaintop vision. Verse 32 confirms the disciples as witnesses to this manifestation of Jesus' glory and to the appearance of Moses and Elijah, even though the three men were tired. The reference to the fatigue provides an explanation for Peter's misguided reaction in v. 33.

Moses and Elijah begin to leave in v. 33, showing that their presence is not permanent. Peter's response, however, moves in the opposite direction. He wants to build them tents so that they have a place to stay. Peter wants to fix and hold something that cannot be held. The building of the tents also evokes the Feast of Tabernacles, a joyous Israelite agricultural festival that celebrates God's bounty towards Israel in the wilderness.

Luke tells the reader that Peter's response is not to be credited ("not knowing what he said"). The correct interpretation of the mountaintop experience is provided by God in vv. 34-35. To the Transfiguration of Jesus is thus added a theophany. The cloud that overshadows all is a powerful figure for the presence of God (see esp. Exod. 16:10; 19:9; 24:15-18; 40:34). This visual theophany is accompanied by a divine pronouncement (v. 35). God's words out of the cloud are a reaffirmation of God's words to Jesus at Jesus' baptism (Luke 3:22). At the baptism, God's words were addressed only to Jesus; now, they are a more public announcement of Jesus' identity, relationship to God, and vocation. The prelude to Jesus' ministry and the prelude to Jesus' passion are thus both marked by God's affirmation of Jesus as God's Son and chosen one (cf. 3:32, "beloved").

The command God gives the disciples, "listen to him," can be linked back to Jesus' words about discipleship in 9:23-27. Jesus' words about discipleship are grounded in God's mandate. The words "listen to him" take on additional meaning when read in the context of v. 36. When the cloud lifts, Moses and Elijah are gone; Jesus stands alone. Jesus' voice has taken the place of the voices of Moses and Elijah as the voice to be heeded. The disciples' silence in v. 36 is further indication that the Transfiguration is to be interpreted in the context of Jesus' passion and death. In 9:21 Jesus commanded his disciples to be silent about his messianic identity, and followed that command with instruction (9:22). The silence of Peter, James, and John here suggests that they do not yet understand enough about Jesus' departure and glory to talk about the Transfiguration. The full meaning of what they have seen will become known to them as Jesus begins his journey to Jerusalem.

Luke thus explicitly links the dramatic manifestation of Jesus' glory at the Transfiguration with the events of Jesus' passion, death, and resurrection. For Luke, Jesus' glory cannot be understood apart from Jesus' suffering, and his suffering cannot be understood apart from his glory. The Lukan version of the Transfiguration thus provides the perfect bridge from a liturgical season that defines itself in terms of the manifestation of light and glory (Epiphany) to the season that moves the church toward Jesus' suffering and death (Lent).

FIRST LESSON: EXODUS 34:29-35

As noted above, each of the four lectionaries emphasizes different aspects of the Transfiguration. The Episcopal and Revised Common Lectionaries have the most texts in common, drawing their Old Testament lesson from Exod. 34:29-35 and their epistle lessons from 1 Corinthians The use of Exod. 34:29-35 highlights the links between the Transfiguration and the Exodus tradition.

In Exodus 32, the people of Israel became impatient during the forty days and nights that Moses was on Mt. Sinai (Exod. 24:15-18) and rebelled against Moses and God by choosing Aaron as their leader and worshiping a golden calf. Moses interceded with God on Israel's behalf (Exodus 33) and God agreed to renew God's covenant with Israel (Exod. 34:1-28). Exodus 34:29-35 narrates Moses' return from Mt. Sinai with new covenant tablets.

This passage contains an interesting interweaving of two themes: the concrete symbol of the renewed covenant (the two stone tablets and God's commandments) and Moses' transfiguration. Each of these themes depicts different dimensions of God's presence in the world and relationship to God's people. In the tablets and the commandments, Israel comes face-to-face with God's will for the conduct of their lives and their relationship to God (vv. 29a, 32, 34b). These commandments, and hence the people's relationship with God, are what the Israelites had broken in worshiping the golden calf. The second theme, Moses' transfiguration, suggests another dimension of relationship with God. Moses' encounter with God on Sinai made the skin of his face shine (v. 29*b*), transforming him in a way of which he was not even aware. Moses' radiance frightened the Israelites (v. 30) because it brought them close to the power and presence of God that transcended their ordinary experience. Moses' radiance was proof that God was indeed present in the covenant. That this radiance did not belong to the ordinary is confirmed by Moses' use of the veil. When he was not communicating God's word to Israel, Moses veiled his face so as not to trivialize the power of God's visible presence. Whenever Moses spoke with God and then spoke God's word to the people, Moses took off his veil (vv. 33-35) so that the radiance was visible. Moses thus brought Israel face-to-face with the glory of God.

The commandments are a reminder of God's imminence, and the transfiguration of Moses points towards God's transcendence. In the interplay of commandment and radiance in Exodus 34, a full portrait of the God of Israel emerges.

SECOND LESSON: 1 CORINTHIANS 13:12—14:2

The expression "face to face" in 1 Corinthians 13:12 establishes the link between the epistle lesson and the Transfiguration (for a fuller discussion of 1 Corinthians 13, see the Fourth Sunday after the Epiphany). Just as Jesus' face was changed as a sign of his glory, and Moses' face shone with God's radiance, the Christian community will also experience transformation in the presence of God. The source of that transformation is God's enduring love.

LUTHERAN FIRST LESSON: DEUTERONOMY 34:1-12

The Lutheran Lectionary, in both its Old Testament and epistle lessons, focuses directly on Moses' experience of God. Deut. 34:1-12 are the closing verses of the Pentateuch and narrate the death of Moses. From the top of Mt. Nebo (v. 1), God shows Moses the promised land, but tells him that he will not cross over (vv. 2-4). Moses dies and is buried in Moab (vv. 5-6). This story has several important connections with the Lukan Transfiguration story. First, the mystery of the location of Moses' burial site (v. 6) contributed to the eschatological expectations that Moses himself might return in the messianic age. Second, the reminder that another prophet like Moses has not arisen (v. 10) also belonged to the Mosaic strand of messianic expectation on which Luke builds in the Transfiguration story. For Luke, Jesus was the expected prophet. Third, Deut. 34:1-12, like the Lukan Transfiguration, combines elements of glory (vv. 10-12) and death (vv. 5-6).

LUTHERAN SECOND LESSON: 2 CORINTHIANS 4:3-6

2 Corinthians 4:3-6 is the conclusion of Paul's parabolic treatment of Moses' experience in Exod. 34:29-35. The full unit is 2 Cor. 3:1—4:6. Paul uses Moses' experience in the presence of God to interpret the Christian's experience of the gospel. Just as Moses veiled his face to prevent the visible radiance of God from overwhelming the Israelites, so does the "god of this world" sometimes veil the light of the gospel to those who are perishing (2 Cor. 4:3-4). The "god of this world" refers to the conflicting loyalties and allegiances that pull one away from God (much like the golden calf in Exod. 32). And just as Moses removed the veil to reveal God's glory to the Israelites, now God has permanently lifted the veil "to give the light of the knowledge of the glory of God in the face of Jesus Christ (2 Cor. 4:6).

ROMAN CATHOLIC FIRST LESSON: DANIEL 7:9-10, 13-14

Daniel 7:9-10, 13-14 supplies the Old Testament lesson for the Roman Catholic Lectionary. This reading highlights the apocalyptic dimensions of the Transfiguration. The images of whiteness and brightness used to describe God ("the Ancient One") in vv. 9-10 belong to the apocalyptic tradition from which the description of Jesus' clothing in Luke 9:29 is drawn. The description of "one like a Son of Man" (NRSV, "one like a human being") in Dan. 7:13 was important in early Christian imagery of Jesus as the Son of Man, as was the description of God's gift to the Son of Man of eternal dominion, glory, and kingship (v. 14). The pairing of Daniel 7 with Luke 9 emphasizes the glory dimension of the Transfiguration.

ROMAN CATHOLIC SECOND LESSON: 2 PETER 1:16-19

2 Peter 1:16-19 contains the only explicit New Testament reference to the Transfiguration that occurs outside the Synoptic Gospels (vv. 17-18). These verses depict the Transfiguration from Peter's perspective ("we," vv. 16b, 18). Regardless of the decision one makes about the pseudonymity of 2 Peter, it is nonetheless true that the letter positions Peter's witness as the theological warrant for what is said. The Transfiguration seems to be cited in vv. 17-18 to support the tradition of Jesus' second coming ("the power and coming of Our Lord Jesus Christ," v. 16). This tradition is not based on "cleverly devised myths," but as vv. 16b-18 show, on the tradition of eyewitnesses. It is not completely clear why the author thought the

Transfiguration supported the tradition of the Second Coming. He may be building his argument this way: If such a manifestation of honor and glory occurred during the first coming (the incarnation), how much more will the honor and glory of the second coming be possible. As with Daniel 7, this reading highlights the glory aspects of the Transfiguration.